INTERNATIONAL DESIGN YEARBOOK 17

Based on an original idea by
Stuart Durant

Chapter introductions by Ross
Lovegrove and commentaries by
Jennifer Hudson

Senior Editor: Cleia Smith
Assistant Editor: Helen McFarland

First published in the United States
of America in 2002 by Abbeville Press
22 Cortlandt Street
New York, NY 10007

First published in Great Britain in
2002 by Laurence King Publishing
71 Great Russell Street
London WC1B 3BP

Copyright © 2002 Laurence King
Publishing

Printed in Hong Kong

First Edition

ISBN 0-7892-0754-0

10 9 8 7 6 5 4 3 2 1

Library of Congress Cataloging-in-
Publication Data available upon
request

Introduction: Peter and Charlotte Fiell
General Editor: Jennifer Hudson
Design: Keith Lovegrove

INTERNATIONAL DESIGN YEARBOOK 17

Edited by Ross Lovegrove

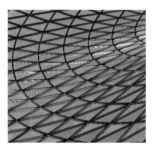

ORGANIC ESSENTIALISM

Peter and Charlotte Fiell

To anyone who is a regular reader of the *International Design Year-book* it will be apparent that a fresh wind of change has swept through the 2002 edition. Upon the suggestion of this year's guest editor, the celebrated industrial designer Ross Lovegrove, the normal product categories have been discarded in favour of five material groupings: metals; glass; textiles; wood and plastics. The primary reason for this is that Lovegrove is first and foremost a materials-led designer who throughout his career has been utterly galvanized by the form-inspiring and often poetic qualities of materials of all different types. It was, therefore, only natural for him to think in terms of materials rather than typologies when it came to categorizing his selection of the previous year's most interesting products. Certainly, his choices and layout help focus attention on the aesthetic, functional and technical potential of both new and familiar materials and their innovative application to designed products today.

To better understand the rationale behind the 2002 selection, it is useful to consider the philosophy that underlies Lovegrove's own work. Over the last decade he has single-handedly pioneered a very distinct approach to design that can be best defined as 'organic essentialism'. To this end, Lovegrove skilfully marries sculptural forms inspired by ergonomics and elements from the natural world (from dinosaur bones to the ribbed structure of a cactus) to a concern for the logical arrangement of only those elements that are absolutely necessary for the accomplishment of a particular purpose. His designs are both anthropocentric and logical, and not only reflect a new naturalism of form that is based fundamentally on the concept of getting the most from the least but exemplify the direction design should be taking for the twenty-first century. Unlike many minimalist designs, which more often than not are style-led and suffer from a rather insipid anorexic quality, Lovegrove's designs are lean yet as shapely as a well-toned body, the innovative and sensually seductive forms lend his products a definable character that in turn gives his clients what they are really looking for – 'distributive uniqueness' – a means by which their products can be strongly differentiated from those by other designers and manufacturers.

Lovegrove's clients can be roughly divided into two camps: those like Tag Heuer who require pure industrial design that can be mass-produced in large numbers and those like Edra who want something more experimental and poetic that can be sold as exclusive limited editions. By working within both the industrial and 'art' design worlds, Lovegrove is able on the one hand to bring craft sensibilities to those products destined for mass manufacture, while on the other to allow industrial know-how to inform his craft-based design. A few of his clients employ a pick-and-mix approach to their selection of designers and engage Lovegrove as a high-profile representative of so-called 'organic design'.

As some manufacturers have found, Ross Lovegrove is not always the easiest designer to work with, just because he is always wanting to push the boat out just that little bit further – whether it be the development of a new materials application, a novel method of production or the subversion of preconceptions about formal and functional attributes of certain typologies. As he puts it, he likes 'to screw around with the potential of perception and colours, while exploring a depth of significance'. In short, while Lovegrove takes the role of design very seriously, he is willing to take risks and expects others to do the same. After all, how else is meaningful progress to be made? The manufacturers who are able to place their whole-hearted faith and trust in Lovegrove often end up with revolutionary products that have a logical clarity of form and a strong physical magneticism – for example, the 'Go' chair for Bernhardt, which possesses both remarkable strength and lightness and is the first chair to be mass-produced in injection-moulded magnesium. When Lovegrove connects with a manufacturer who fully commits to his vision, the results can be almost alchemic as well as deeply satisfying to the senses. It can, however, often take a huge effort and a certain amount of frustration to reach this goal as Lovegrove categorically refuses to compromise

Mineral water bottle
Blow moulded PET
Ty Nant, Wales

on production values and, ultimately, quality. It is this aspect of his personality, however, that ensures that his products remain distinct from all others.

From kitchen utensils and cutlery to furniture and lighting, Lovegrove's designs are also notable for their exquisite detailing – the way they fit so comfortably in the hand or delight the eye with their subtle gestural lines. Lovegrove is probably one of the most gifted draftsmen in the design industry today, and his constant sketching allows him to refine his ideas and visions to a very high degree before they are worked up by his studio assistants into three-dimensional computer images or resin stereolithography models. Indeed, watching him sketch with such rapid fluidity, it can seem as if he has his own 'superhighway' connecting his brain to his hand. This remarkable ability, which he uses methodologically, enables him to efficiently conceptualize and develop connections of many different types. Indeed, it could be said that Lovegrove earns his living foremost by making innovative and completely unexpected connections between objects, materials, functions and people.

Like sculptures by Henry Moore or Isamu Noguchi, Lovegrove's designs reflect something of the abstract essence of nature and possess an engaging tactility that invites physical interaction. His work has a remarkable sensitivity born of a deep respect (or *hari* as it is known in Japan) for the materials with which he works. As he succinctly explains, 'Designers must value the materials that they work with as precious resources whether they are natural or synthetic.' Through his work, he tries to emulate the quiet nobility or 'silent culture' of Japanese design and attempts to express an inherent material honesty. Lovegrove's search for the elusive poetry of Japanese design – the soul of an object, or as he puts it, 'the Kuramata presence' – is powerfully reflected in the sculptural values and refined detailing of his work. He reveres the ability of Japanese culture to synthesize the old with the new and is fully aware of the powerful synergy that is created when the traditional meets the contemporary head on. A powerful

example of this is Tokujin Yoshioka's house on the outskirts of Tokyo, where modern industrial materials dramatically contrast with the age-old structure of a traditional Japanese building.

Lovegrove is constantly searching for state-of-the-art materials that will enable him to 'find the sculptural line of things that exist in the natural world'. He takes an almost childlike delight in the properties of new synthetic materials, from foamed aluminium to Kevlar, often repeating the word 'amazing' in his sheer wonder at the formal and structural potential these materials offer him. As he handles materials like these, his imagination runs wild with 'what ifs' – this being the seed from which truly innovative and remarkable material applications very often evolve. He is equally captivated by and enthusiastic about advanced production technologies that will allow him to bring a freshness of ideas and real improvement to his design solutions. Against this fascination with synthetic materials and cutting-edge industrial processes, Lovegrove also has a great love of natural materials such as bamboo and wood, as well as age-old craft skills, from wickerwork to lacquer. Frequently, these traditional materials and ancient manufacturing techniques inform his work and stimulate elegant contemporary applications.

Above all else it is the forms and structures found in the natural world that inspire Lovegrove. The shape of his new plastic water bottle for Ty Nant, for example, was informed by his investigations into the flow patterns that occur when water is poured. Often when he is giving a presentation, he will intersperse images of his design work with images of the natural forms that inspired them, from jellyfish and plant leaves to blood cells. As he has observed, 'There is an absolute beauty in organic forms that stimulate deeply within the subconscious. I am moved by the honesty and richness of such forms which celebrate the three-dimensional effect of our living in harmony with space.'

Lovegrove's innate pantheism has bred a strong dislike of materialistic decadence – he abhors the irresponsible use of precious

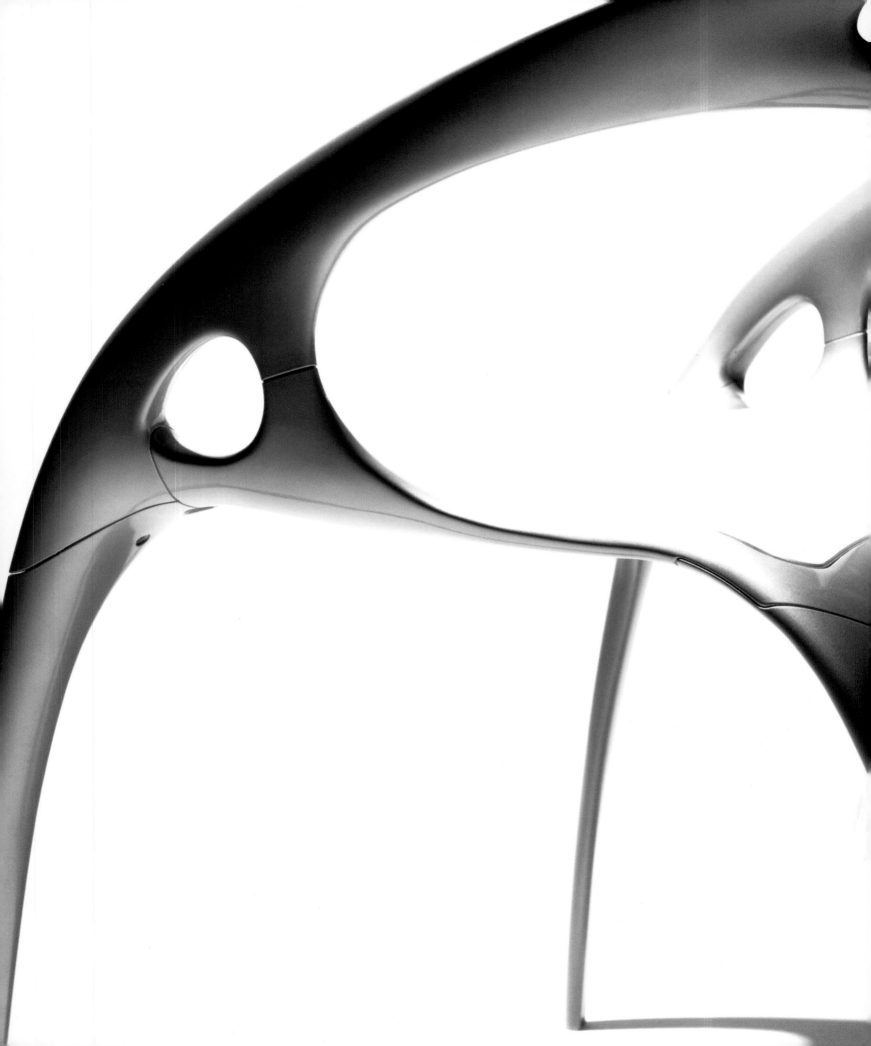

resources and distrusts anything that fuels functional and stylistic obsolescence and the needless production of waste. At the same time, he promotes the notion of product durability – functional and aesthetic longevity – because by making things last longer their net environmental impact can be radically reduced. Some of Lovegrove's work can be seen as evolutionary reworkings of well-known design classics that have stood the test of time, such as Arne Jacobsen's famous '3107' chair. These are neither homages to the past nor a bid to jump on the retro bandwagon, but earnest attempts at reinterpreting ideal forms within a contemporary industrial and material context. Whether a design is mass-produced or a one-off, Lovegrove seeks to unify art and design through solutions that are preferably process-driven.

The selection of work chosen by Lovegrove on the following pages reveals not only a highly positive belief in the future but also an exacting eye that is stimulated by the pioneering use of new forms, functions, materials and production techniques. He is similarly excited by the intellectual and physical bringing together of seemingly disparate materials, from wood and carbon fibre to plastics and bamboo, for such contrasts often emphasize more dramatically the materials' intrinsic qualities. This year's choice of designs also demonstrates Lovegrove's interest in the continuing cross-pollination of disciplines and his belief that craft-based and industrially produced designs have equal validity. Above all, it is innovation that has been the decisive factor in determining what products should be included in this annual survey of design. It would seem that innovation and experimentation most often emerge from the craft workshop rather than the industrialized factory, from the search for individualistic rather than universal solutions. As Lovegrove acknowledges, 'craft is the melting pot into which industry gazes'. There appears in today's society a place as much for craft-based low-tech individualistic solutions as for mass-produced hi-tech universally appealing solutions – the two worlds of design can live in harmony, learning from and thriving off one another.

Since the beginning of civilization materials have shaped our cultural identity – from the Stone Age to the Iron Age to the Plastics Age. In the future, 'to-die-for' strong yet super-lightweight metal alloys such as nickel-titanium and aluminium-magnesium will allow designers to get more mileage out of less material use thereby minimizing the mass of objects. The perpetual development of advanced composite materials will also increasingly offer new design potential as they meld surface with structure. So-called 'techno' polymers will similarly promote new ways of making things, while existing technologies such as rotational moulding and gas-injection moulding will be refined so as to provide yet more efficient and inexpensive ways of producing objects in plastics. The materials and technologies of the future, many of which are represented in the *Yearbook*, will ultimately enable designers on the one hand to create a more individualistic and expressive language of design, while on the other hand allow them to develop better performing, more anthropocentric universal solutions. As has been repeatedly demonstrated throughout modern history, ultra-advanced 'futuristic' materials inevitably find innovative product applications that push the formal, functional and aesthetic parameters of design to new and extraordinary limits. This year's Lovegrove selection offers an inspirational and well-informed taste of what is to come ... enjoy!

'Go' chair
High pressure injection-moulded magnesium
Bernhardt Design, USA

FUSING BOUNDARIES

Ross Lovegrove

We have begun the twenty-first century with a memory of the twentieth that lingers by virtue of a revisionary perspective that is quite natural for a new generation trying to create within an emerging climate of complexity. Ideas are now hyper-exposed and freely exchanged between disciplines, thus creating a new hybrid mutant culture without rules or preconceptions. This constant breaking-down and rebuilding of possibilities is nowhere more evident than in the fashion industry, which is by far the most vital influence on our present creative energies. As a commercial art form, fashion design successfully combines the hard and the soft, the industrial and the artisanal all within an intensely self-perpetuating atmosphere of relentless innovation.

There is a new relationship emerging between fashion designers and architects that is carrying this atmosphere of innovation into the built environment. The work of Herzog & de Meuron, Rem Koolhaas and Future Systems, to name a few of the best known, is blurring our perceptions of the boundaries between art and technology, form and construction, a path that Issey Miyake so uniquely pioneered. In parallel, one can begin to see the absorption of architectural languages into the world of automotive design, by definition an industry akin to architecture in its use of materials, definition of space and the time frames required to construct and visualize. Architecture and automotive design share a common platform in that they contribute the most to the quality of our shared urban environment, exchanging values that go beyond the purely visual into the potential realms of intelligent use of resources and self-sustaining systems.

We are seeing a new kind of architecture arise that has clear product qualities, for example Nicholas Grimshaw's Eden Project, which fuses nature with polymer technology, or the ABB Architects' BMW Pavilion in Munich, which points towards the creation of an automotively inspired, anatomically smooth architecture for our new urban horizon. On a smaller and more intimate scale, products can be seen to be influencing – from a formal, material and technological point of view – the way things are conceived at a more complex level.

To manufacture products such as consumer durables in the vast quantities required today, technology must be pushed to its limits to deliver ever greater levels of economy and functional reliability. To create with simplicity, one must first understand the complexities of the equation that determines the optimum alignment of factors to arrive at a successful product of universal value. This is the scenario that the automotive industry faces every day, one that is further complicated by the serious impact that cars have on our environment in terms of noise and air pollution – a sad reality that seems to undo the positive aspects of their contribution to our everyday dependence on mobility.

Cars need a radical new rethink in order to evolve, and many of the clues to their future success, both culturally and commercially, lie in the economies of product design – its reductive principles towards componentry and straightforwardness of material expression. If we can learn to accept that cars in an urban situation should not be driven at more than 15 mph, then they can happily be made like a set of large plastic suitcases. Equally, if we can be humble enough to accept that their bodies do not need to be glossy and painted, then once again plastics in their most industrialized forms combined with fibrous additives could replace metals as the industry standard. Plastics allow for the serious reduction of components and a wonderful synergy between design and engineering.

Indeed, clever use of the characteristics employed every day in the field of consumer products such as live hinges, co-injection of hard and soft polymers, gas injection and so on can improve with ever greater levels of efficiency those working characteristics that are common to all car types. With such methods, cars would become lighter, more robust, less precious, more fuel-efficient and ultimately very cool status symbols for those who value the car as a practical tool for urban living. The car is a link between the special world of architecture and the tactile world of the product and as such is a key link in the seamless connection between home and the environment. Because of this it will absorb influences from all directions,

Biowood sculpture
Ceccotti, Italy

evolving in response to highly personal, highly communal and highly global issues.

Monitoring the evolution of the car will give a strong indication of the state of humanity as a whole from a social, technological and ethical perspective. It is important to be aware of why certain things have evolved in the way they have or why they evolved in the first place in order to better understand their essence and to then re-evaluate them within a contemporary context. The richness and aesthetic diversity acquired through constant reassessment and experimentation is the most vital contributor to progress, whether for industrial or artistic purposes. Today there is a new spirit of material use that is multi-inspirational and joyful to a new generation who have an increasing capacity to absorb ideas and attitudes that are born out of ever more opposing and complex viewpoints.

METALS

Metallurgy – the science and technology of metals and their alloys – is opening up many new possibilities in terms of the technological transfer between creative disciplines. Above all, automobile manufacture, with its reproductive precision, resourcefulness and emphasis on the relationship between strength and lightness, is increasingly stimulating architects' and designers' investigations into the way certain structures are conceived and produced. But for every industry that is advancing mass production through the economics of scale, there is a counterpart using methods that are more open to experimentation. Superform aluminium, for example, is employed not only by such well-established companies as Aston Martin but also by Biomega, a new brand that through relatively modest investment has been able to exploit this material to gain worldwide recognition.

In this section I have juxtaposed projects in a deliberate way, playfully suggesting the influence one might have had or could have on the other. Of particular note is the plated leaf by Ann Pamintuan of the Philippines, the sensual beauty of which conveys emotions that are so rarely felt in our industrially clinical world. In parallel, the pressed aluminium BMW component by Tokujin Yoshioka makes us aware that seemingly dry industrial engineering solutions have their own kind of honest beauty, in which man-made and artificial worlds are made to unite. When passed through the sensitive mind of someone like Tokujin, these materials take on a heightened value, so that even the very humblest can be made to describe new and unexpected ways of defining space.

Marcel Wanders
Flower chair
Matt chromed steel
h. 64cm (25in) w. 78cm (30³⁄₈in)
d. 71cm (27⁷⁄₈in)
Mooi, the Netherlands

Ann Pamintuan
Brooch, Eyelet leaf
Fresh eyelet leaf gilded in gold,
silver and copper
Dimensions depend on leaf
The Gilded Expressions, the Philippines

Ann Pamintuan, a member of
Movement 8 in the Philippines,
describes her creations as 'expressions of life's raw elegance'. As a
traditional Philippine housewife,
she enrolled in ikebana and bonsai classes. Disheartened by the
fact that her creations were
inevitably transient, she took the
radical step of taking a course in
electroplating. She experimented
on insects, fruits and even a green

snake before producing a line of
exclusive jewellery for a boutique
on New York's 5th Avenue.
Gradually her hobby has turned
into an industry. Bangles and
brooches formed from electroplat-
ed orchid roots finished in gold,
silver and copper are the inspiration behind her 'Cocoon Wire
Furniture', which is welded and
hammered by hand and retains its
natural rusty look (see page 20).

16

Tamar Ben David
Oval tray, centrepiece and tray;
Idro, Ledro, Lario
Pewter
Idro: h. 3cm (1 1/8in) w. 43cm (16 3/4in)
d. 20cm (7 7/8in)
Ledro: h. 5cm (2in) di. 30cm (11 7/8in)
Lario: h. 3cm (1 1/8in) w. 60cm (23 3/8in)
d. 12cm (4 5/8in)
Serafino Zani srl, Italy

Kazuhiko Tomita
Knife and fork, Morode
Stainless steel
w. 1.9cm (3/4in) l. 22.5cm (8 7/8in)
Covo srl, Italy

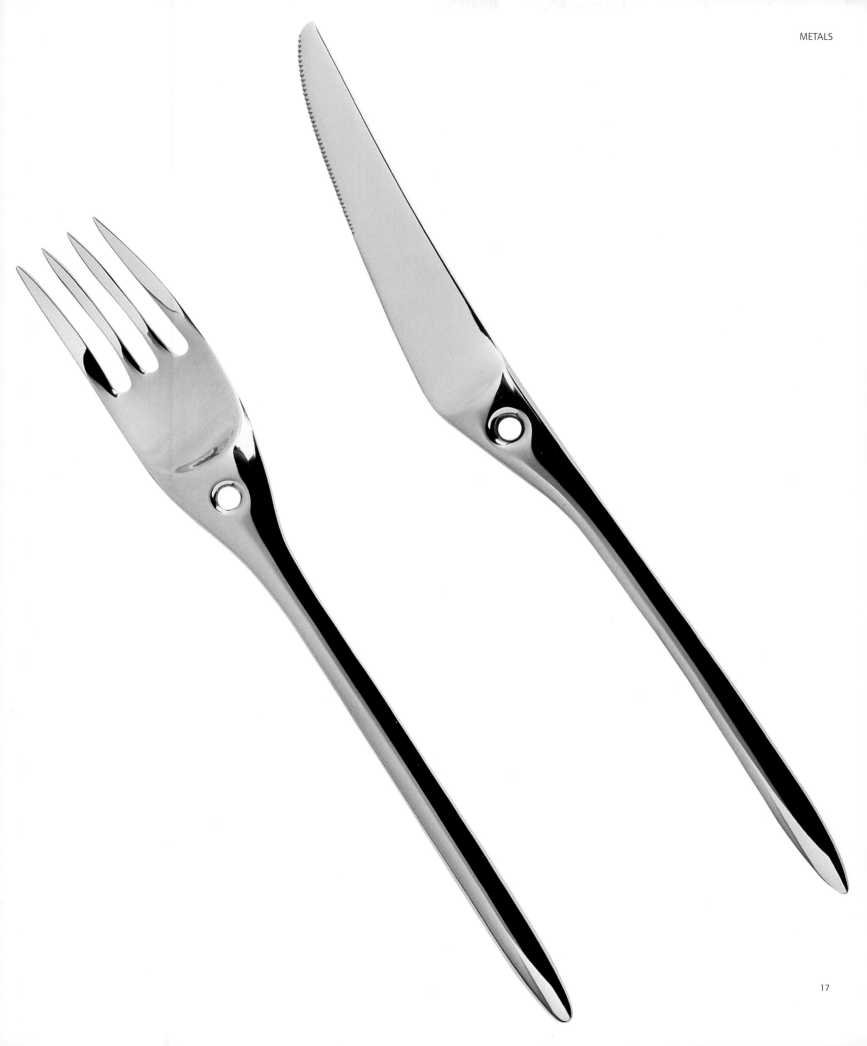

LEFT
David Huycke
Vase, Ovalinder 2
Silver
h. 17cm (6¾in) di. 10/13cm (4/5⅛in)
Limited batch production

ABOVE
David Huycke
Vases, Bolinder 3
Cast silver
h. 16cm (6⅜in) di. 10cm (4in)
Limited batch production

Ann Pamintuan
Cocoon chair
Wire
h. 74cm (28⁷⁄₈in) w. 74cm (28⁷⁄₈in)
d. 86.5cm (33¾in)
The Gilded Expressions, the Philippines

Antonio Citterio
Chair, Iuta
Die cast aluminium, mesh
h. 80cm (31¼in) w. 61cm (23⅜in)
B&B Italia, Italy

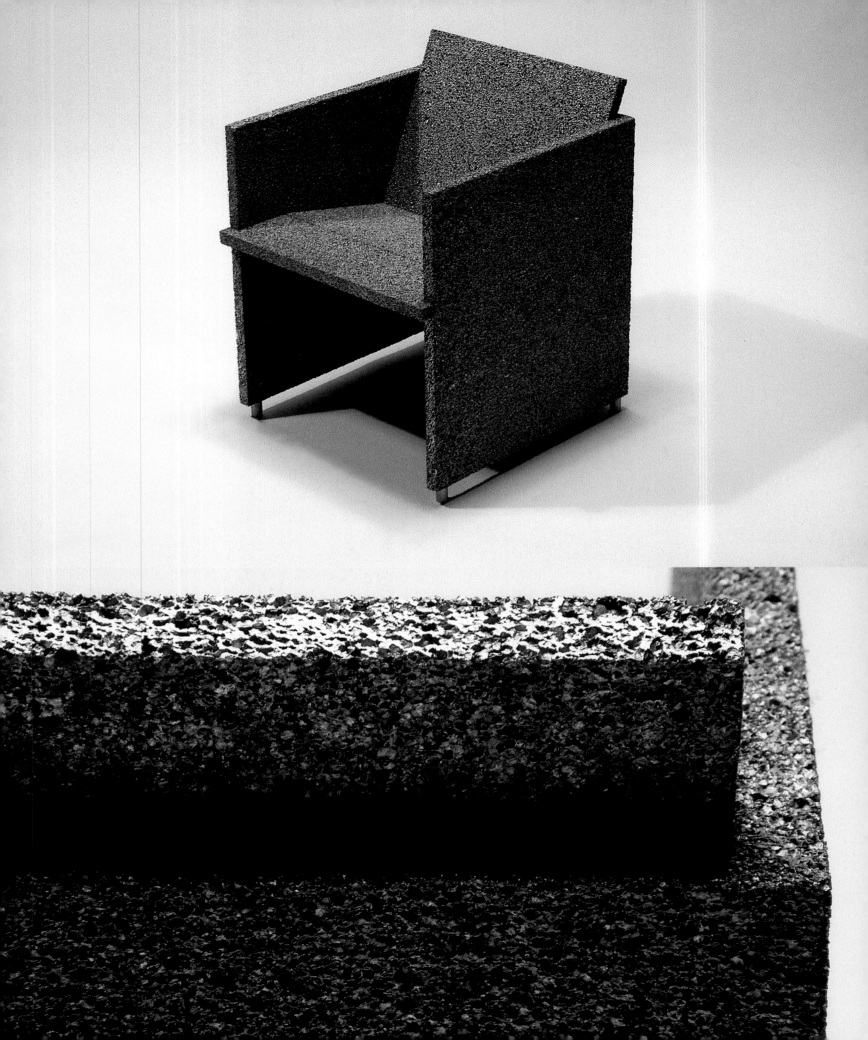

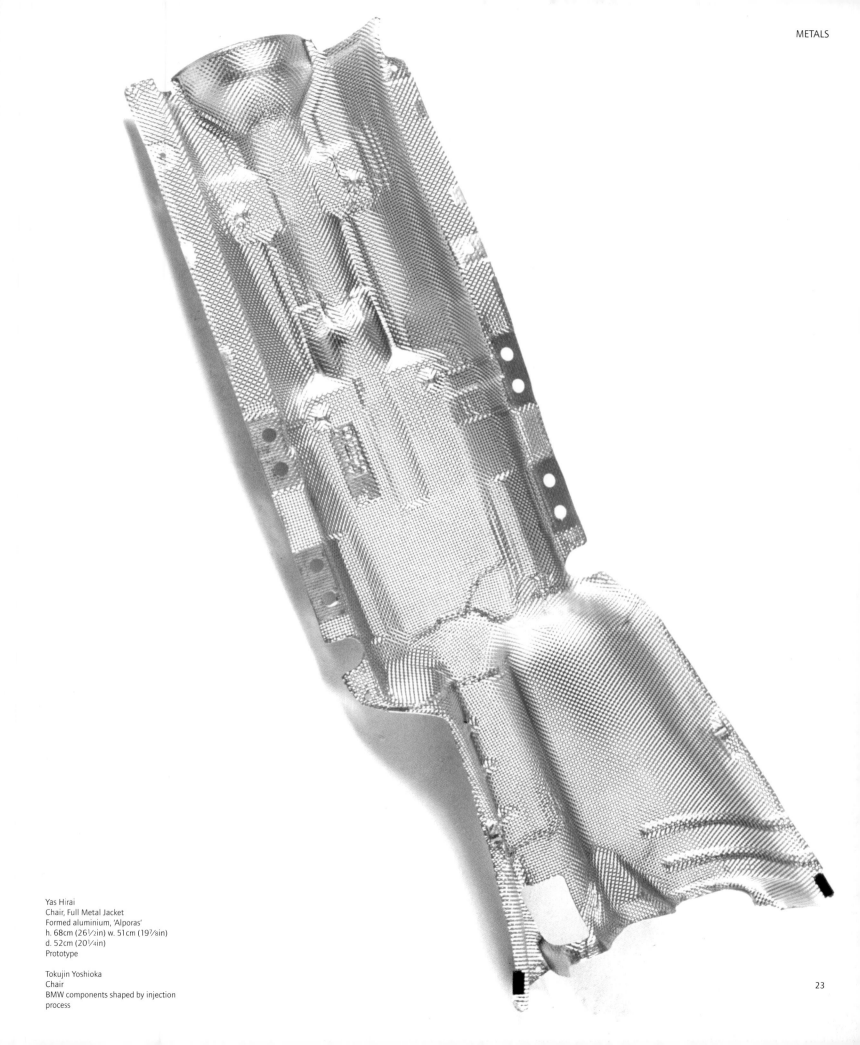

Yas Hirai
Chair, Full Metal Jacket
Formed aluminium, 'Alporas'
h. 68cm (26½in) w. 51cm (19⅞in)
d. 52cm (20¼in)
Prototype

Tokujin Yoshioka
Chair
BMW components shaped by injection
process

T. Tanaka, Y. Shibata, M. Kamegi
Notebook PC, DynaBook SSS
Magnesium alloy
h. 3.4cm (1³/₈in) w. 27cm (10⁵/₈in)
l. 24.5cm (9⁵/₈in)
Toshiba Corporation, Japan

Audi A2
Aluminium body
h. 155.3cm (60¹/₂in) w. 167.3cm
(65³/₈in) l. 382.6cm (149¹/₂in)
Audi AG, Germany

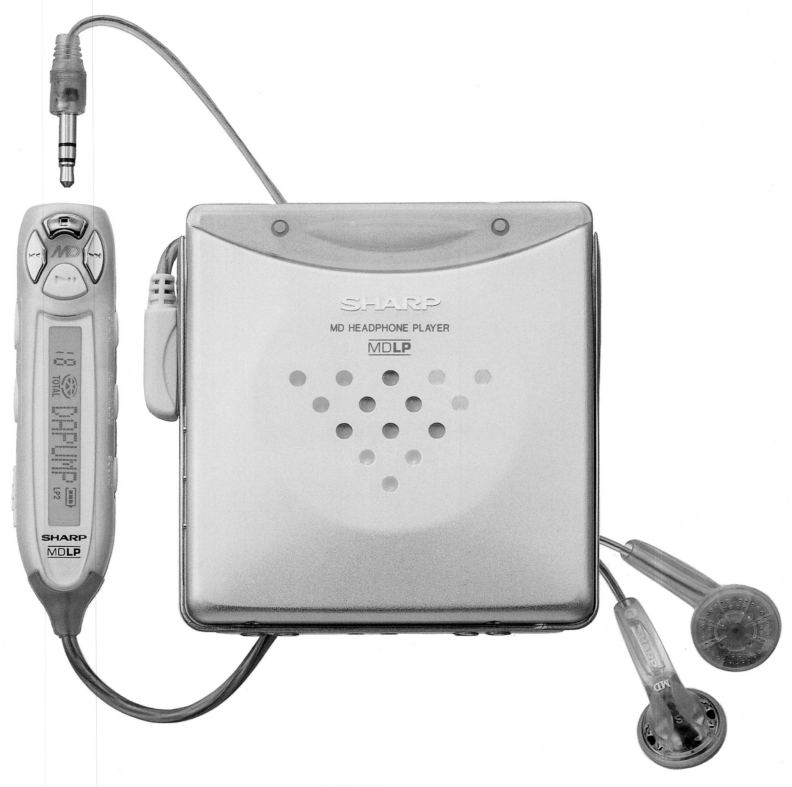

Yasuhiko Miyoshi
Portable minidisc player, MD-ST70
Aluminium, acrylic, iron, ABS, PS
h. 8cm (3 1/8in) w. 7.4cm (2 7/8in)
d. 1.6cm (5/8in)
Sharp Corporation, Japan

Therefore Design
Ace multi-screen communicator
Anodized aluminium
l. 6cm (2 3/8in) w. 6cm (2 3/8in) d. 1.6cm
(5/8in) closed
l. 12cm (4 5/8in) w. 12cm (4 5/8in)
d. 1.6cm (5/8in) open
Prototype

Ferdinand Porsche,
Christian Schwamkrug
Digital still camera, FinePix 6800
and 4800
Aluminium, magnesium
h. 9.8cm (3⅞in) w. 8cm (3⅛in)
d. 3.6cm (1⅜in)
Fuji Photo Film Co. Ltd, Japan

DESIGN BY F·A·PORSCHE

OPTICAL 3x ZOOM f=8.3~24.9mm

FUJIFILM

DIGITAL CAMERA

FinePix 4800 Zoom

SUPER CCD

Helle Damkjær
Ashtray, Uno
Polished stainless steel
h. 6.5cm (2½in) w. 12.5cm (4⅞in)
1. 12.5cm (4⅞in)
Rosendahl A∕S, Denmark

Marc Newson
Torch, Apollo
Aluminium, plastic, leather
l. 5.6cm (2¼in) di. 2.4cm (1in)
Flos, Italy

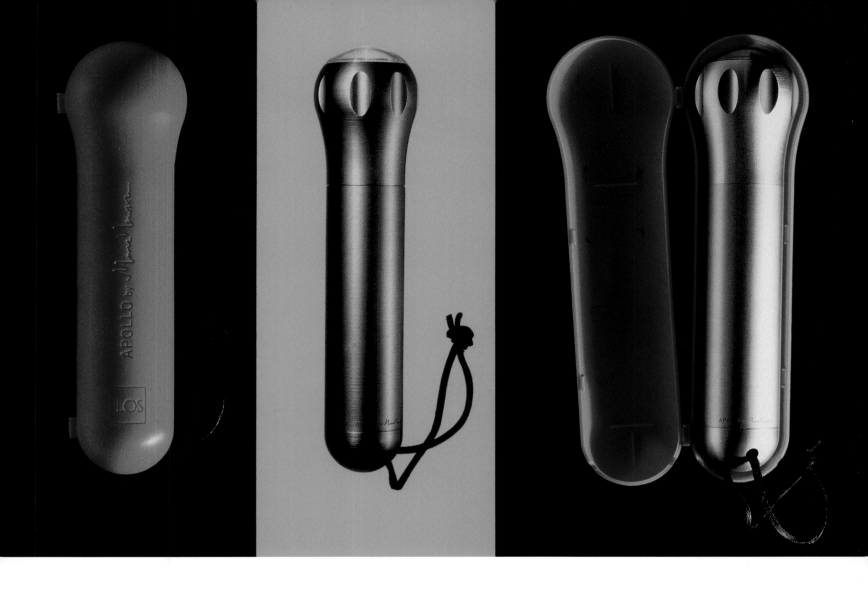

Gijs Bakker is probably best known as the co-founder of Droog Design, although for the last few years he has mainly been involved in creating innovative products for leading international companies. His sense of observation and creative poetry have resulted in a range of table accessories called 'Flow'. Noting the shape and shading of a drop of falling water, he has translated his observations into a series of products in which the sensuously curved surfaces of the two constituent materials – glass and stainless steel – merge with one another into a harmonious whole. So far the range consists of a fruit bowl, a salad bowl and serving set, a cheese dome, a carafe set and oil and vinegar bottles. He intends to explore different materials in future designs in the range.

A&E Design
Door handles, Habo
Brass, chromium plated
h. 4.5cm (1¾in) w. 2cm (¾in)
l. 12cm (4⅝in)
Isaksson Gruppen AB, Denmark

Foster and Partners
Shower mixer and bath mixer tap
Satined chrome
Rubinetterie Stella SpA, Italy

Gijs Bakker
Tableware, Flow
Stainless steel, glass
Various sizes
Van Kempen & Begeer, the Netherlands

OVERLEAF
Michele De Lucchi
Table lamp, Sempronio
Aluminium, zanak
72 white LEDs
h. 57cm (22½in) w. 19.5cm (7⅝in)
d. 51–84cm (20⅛–33⅛in)
Artemide SpA, Italy

Christoph Behling
Outdoor light, Solargrass
Polycarbonate, solarmodule, ultrabright
LEDs, stainless steel
h. 600–800cm (234–312in)
di. 120cm (46⅞in)
Kopf Solardesign/Regiolux

33

H. Nakano, T. Takada
Washer dryer, TW-F70
Steel, PP ABS
h. 85cm (33½in) w. 64cm (25⅜in)
d. 63.9cm (25⅛in)
Toshiba Corporation, Japan

Dyson
Double drum washing machine,
Contrarotator™
Polycarbonate, galvanized steel,
anti-magnetic stainless alloy
h. 84.8cm (33in) w. 59.5cm (23¼in)
d. 57.5cm (22½in)
Dyson Ltd, UK

Casimir
Chair, Alu Chair
Welded 4mm aluminium sheet
h. 74cm (29⅛in) w. 74cm (29⅛in)
l. 74cm (29⅛in)
Casimir, Belgium

Sam Hecht/IDEO
Dishwasher, Bellagio
Stainless steel, natural butadine
rubber
h. 81.5cm (31⅞in) w. 60cm (23⅜in)
d. 58cm (22⅝in)
LGE, Korea

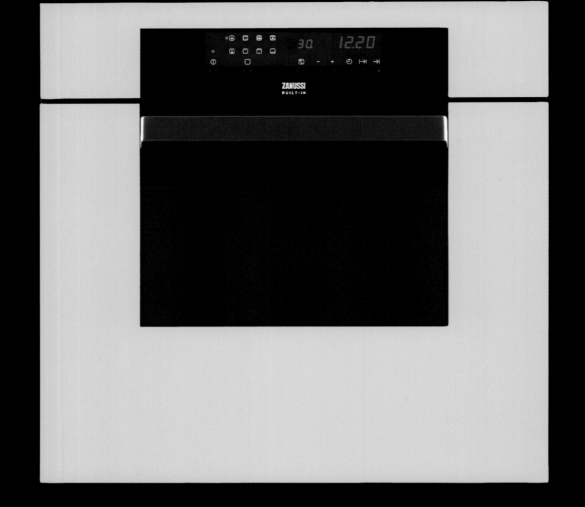

Roberto Pezzetta
Oven, Aluminium
Black glass, aluminium
h. 82cm (32³⁄₈in) w. 60cm (23⁵⁄₈in)
d. 55.5cm (21⁷⁄₈in)
Electrolux Zanussi SpA, Italy

Piero Lissoni
Modular Storage System, Avio
Dolufolex aluminium
Various sizes
Cappellini SpA, Italy

GLASS

We often think of glass merely as decorative and forget its utility as a precision material used on a massive global scale. In the automotive sector around 1800 million units of glass are used in the United States alone every year. Glass is without question one of the world's most vital materials, possessing almost magical properties that afford us not only transparency but thermal and solar protection. Its architectural applications are already vast and are rapidly expanding. Pilkington's development of a new surface coating that makes glass self-cleaning, along with other advances in three-dimensional forming technology and bonding techniques, will help us conceive and construct buildings with a more product-like purpose, thereby making our skylines more organic and optically interactive.

Artificial display technology, which is already integrated into society on a massive scale, and transportation and architecture as methods of communication will begin to be blended seamlessly wherever glass is employed. Thin-film technology, coatings and hybridization with polymers will help support new integrated and pollution-free energy sources that are more durable and informal, so that cars, for example, can become more essential while at the same time providing the user with a higher degree of individualism in terms of their graphic adaptation. The creative potential of such ideas will further blur the boundaries between disciplines, as all types of larger-scale objects seen in our urban environment become more visually adaptive through liquid-crystal surfacing and optical properties. The overall result will be less dense, lighter and more holistically integrated cities.

ABOVE
Takahide Sano
Glass decanter, Kemushi (Hairy Worm)
Blown borosilicate glass
h. 17cm (6⅝in) l. 34cm (13¼in)
d. 9cm (3½in)
Massimo Lunardon & C. SNC, Italy
Limited batch production

FACING
Takahide Sano
Glass decanter, Mickey
Blown borosilicate glass
h. 26cm (10⅛in) l. 34cm (13¼in)
d. 13cm (5⅛in)
Massimo Lunardon & C. SNC, Italy
Limited batch production

Fully connected: all the parts
of the 'Mickey' and 'Kemushi'
decanters are joined together,
allowing the wine to move freely
within each.

Roderick Vos/Design Studio Maupertuus
Table glass from series of 12 objects,
Generation X (homage to A.D. Copier)
Glass
Smallest: h. 6.5cm (2½in) di. 8cm
(3⅛in)
Largest: h. 34cm (13¼in) di. 4cm
(1½in)
Royal Leerdam Crystal, the Netherlands
Prototypes

Fernando and Humberto Campana
Vase, Bataque Vase
Glass
h. 47cm (18½in) w. 43cm (17in)
l. 50cm (19¾in)
Studio Campana, Brazil

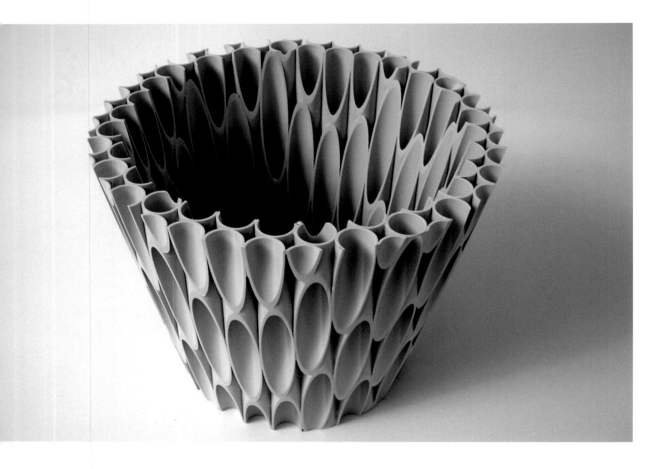

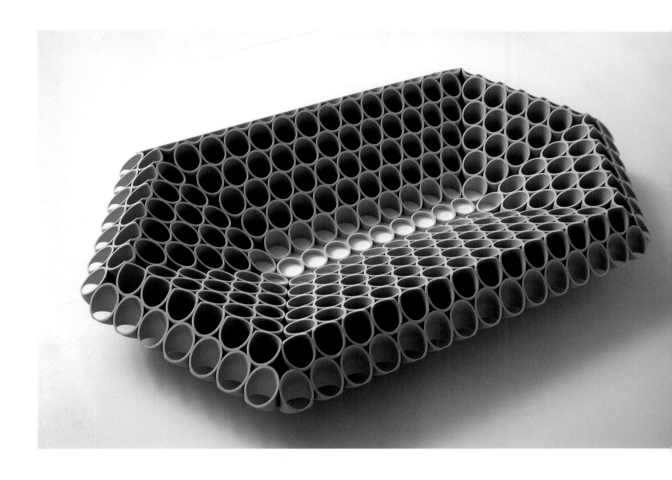

Delo Lindo
Bucket, Contenants
PVC tubes
h. 25cm (9³/₄in) di. 30cm (11³/₄in)
Limited batch production

Delo Lindo
Plate, Contenants
PVC tubes
h. 9cm (3¹/₂in) w. 34cm (13¹/₄in)
l. 56cm (21⁷/₈in)
Limited batch production

Alberto Meda
Carafe, Water
Vitreous china, stainless steel
Jug: 1l Glass: 35cl
Tray: di. 38cm (15in)
Arabia, Finland

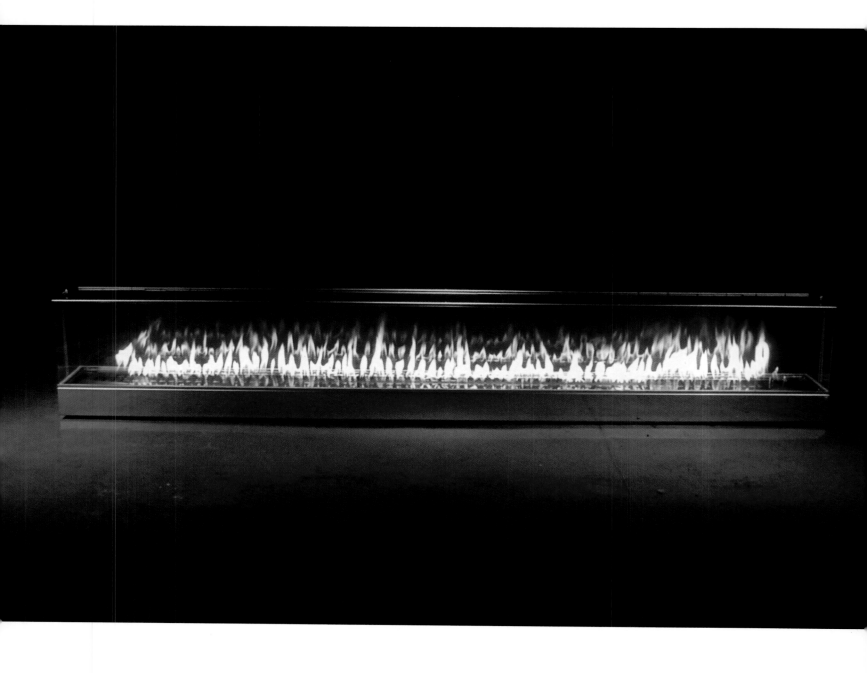

Timo Salli
Fire, Firebox
Ceramic glass, stainless steel, filter
h. 40cm (15⁵⁄₈in) l. 250cm (97¹⁄₂in)
w. 25cm (9³⁄₄in)
Muotoilutoimisto Salli Ltd, Finland
Prototype

Marco Romanelli
Sixties Lighting Pouf,
Wooden frame with stress resistant
polyurethane foam and polyester fibre,
fluorescent bulb
Small: l. 70cm (27⁵/₈in) d. 40cm
(15³/₄in)
Medium: l. 90cm (35¹/₂in) d. 90cm
(35 ¹/₂in)
Large: l. 140cm (55¹/₈in) d. 70cm
(27⁵/₈in)
Ferlea, Italy
Limited Batch Production

OVERLEAF
Yves Béhar
LCD windows, Mind Room
Liquid crystal display, glass
h. 120in (46⁷/₈in) w. 180in (70¹/₄in)
l. 20cm (7³/₄in)
Prototype

Yves Béhar's 'Mind Room' lets the
imagination roam and challenges
the definitional boundaries
between wallpaper, space, landscape and technology. Liquid
crystal displays show varying
scenes in different transparencies
either on command or using a
random pattern, emptying the
mind and allowing it to wander
and daydream.

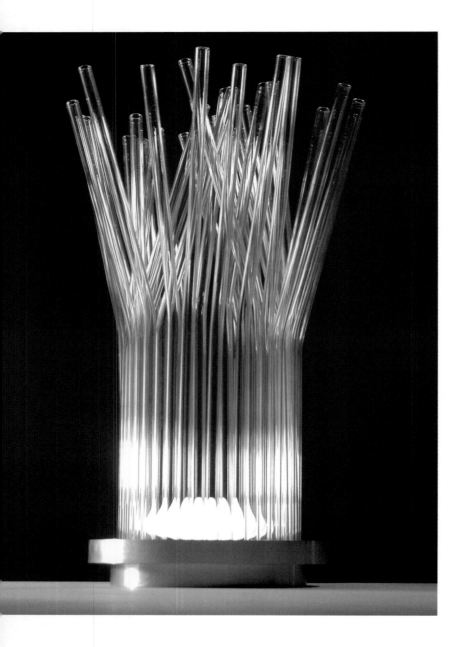

Each of the forty transparent Pyrex tubes used in 'Fluxus' can rotate through 360 degrees, producing many different configurations from the same lamp. Since winning the Satellite prize at the 2000 Milan Furniture Fair, Ulian has been taken up by various leading manufacturers, who recognize in his work the right blend of technical expertise, experimentation and poetry. He is not interested in the merely elegant, but needs his designs to go that little bit further. He does not like to copy or reinterpret but to find fresh means of arriving at a concept: 'It is precisely by following non-linear paths that you can achieve the definition of a good design.' He is very interested in materials and often sits an example on his desk for weeks on end, looking, feeling, questioning: 'Many of my objects are born by observing and manipulating new or traditional materials, by understanding totally their individual qualities. Through this process I sometimes discover – often accidentally – hidden properties or unexpected applications.'

Paolo Ulian
Table lamp, Fluxus
Aluminium, Pyrex
150w bulb
h. 60cm (23½in) di. 27cm (10½in)
Luminara, Italy

Ingegerd Råman
Vase cylinder, Slowfox
Crystal
h. 22.5cm (8⅞in) w. 20cm (7⅞in)
Orrefors Kosta Boda AB, Sweden

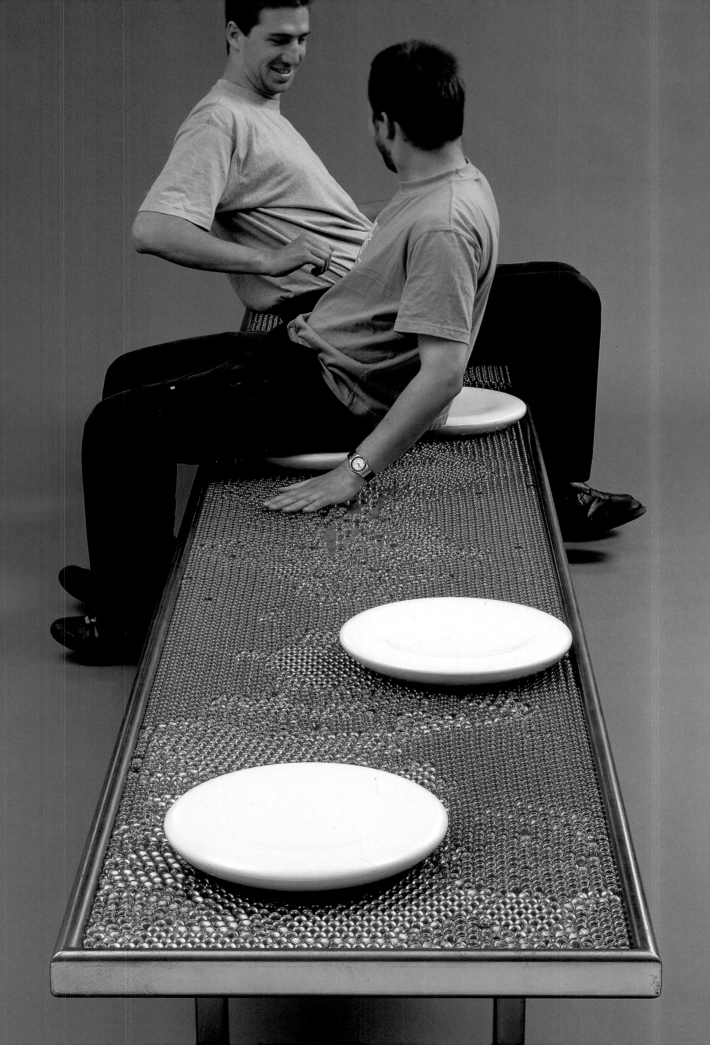

Nina Farkache
Bench, Come a little bit closer
Steel, glass marbles, MDF
h. 43cm (17in) l. 460cm (181¼in)
d. 68cm (26¾in)
Droog Design, the Netherlands

Always thought-provoking yet often tongue-in-cheek, Droog Design's new collection is entitled 'Me, Myself and You' – a series of objects that either encourage or discourage participation. We have all experienced being in the wrong place at the wrong time, being in a crowded room but wanting to fade into the background, or wishing you could introduce yourself at a party but not having an opening gambit. Next Design has created garden fences that would make ignoring your neighbours almost impossible, whereas its 'Key Hole' and 'Spy Hole' doors are enough to keep out both friend and foe – only one hole works. Nina Farkache's bench, 'Come a little bit closer', is an absolute joy – users can just slide together discreetly and smoothly across a bed of marbles.

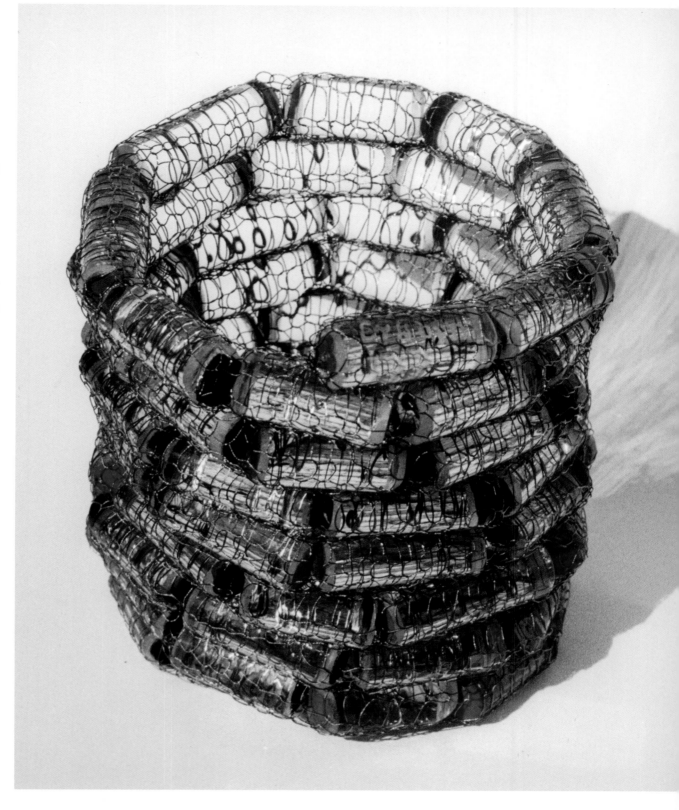

Uta Majmudar
Cylindrical Vessel
Painted glass rods, stainless steel net
h. 14cm (5½in) w. 14cm (5½in)
l. 14cm (5½in)
One-off

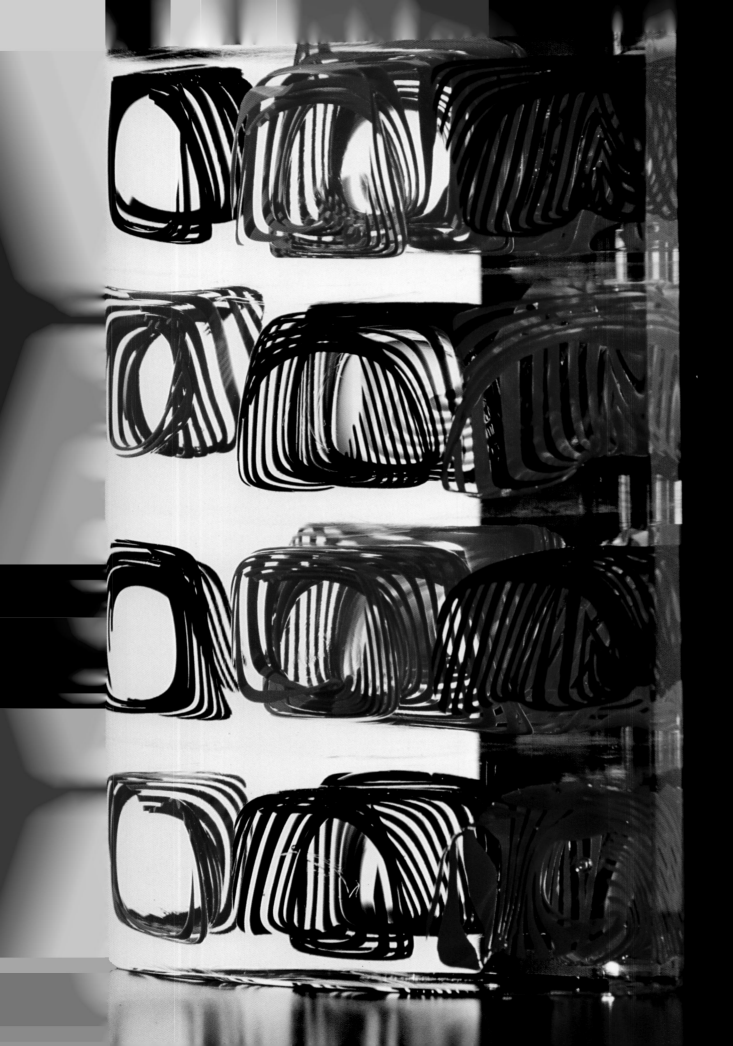

Carlo Moretti
Table object, Monolith Zanfirico 12.c
Murano crystal
h. 18cm (7¼in) w. 13cm (5⅛in)
d. 5.3cm (2⅛in)
Carlo Moretti srl, Italy
Limited batch production

Carlo Moretti's Murano crystal
Monolith comprises twelve
monoblocks, each made in a
different coloured zanfirico.
The monoblocks are first of
all individually squared up and
ground down, then fused together
to form a single piece of crystal,
which is then ground with a sand-
stone wheel in order to achieve
the final shape.

Massimo Micheluzzi
Bowl
Murrina glass
h. 18cm (7in) w. 10cm (4in) di. 29cm
(11³⁄8in)
One-off

Italian designer Massimo
Micheluzzi's pieces are graphic
works in three dimensions. He
was brought up in Venice and
collaborates with traditional
master craftsmen, deriving his
inspiration from the city's magical
landscape and in particular the
play of light on water, old stone
and salt-veined brick.

Marcel Wanders
Crystal vase, Splinter
Crystal
h. 15cm (5⁷⁄8in) w. 15cm (5⁷⁄8in)
d. 15cm (5⁷⁄8in)
Mooi, the Netherlands

Johanna Grawunder
Vase, Cordone
Hand blown/modelled glass
h. 31cm (12¹⁄4in) w. 18cm (7in)
Salviati, Italy
Limited batch production

OVERLEAF
Johanna Grawunder
Centrepiece, Riccio
Transparent blown glass with external
glass bubbles
h. 15cm (5⁷⁄8in) di. 37cm (14³⁄8in)
Salviati, Italy

One of Ingo Maurer's earliest creations was a vase, but so long have we associated the designer with poetic, ethereal and theatrical lighting designs and installations that it comes as somewhat of a surprise to find his name among the three people invited by Salviati to design hand blown Murano glassware. (The other two are American: Ted Muehling, who designs jewellery and decorative objects, and architect Johanna Grawunder.) Although Maurer was asked to reinterpret a medium with which he is relatively unfamiliar, he succeeded in producing a series of sculptural pieces of striking beauty. He 'enjoyed working with the old masters tremendously', although he found the process complicated and the glass unpredictable: 'Glass has a life of its own, I wanted to touch it and bend it, but of course I could not. I was creating in my mind and was entirely dependent on somebody else.' Since his appointment as artistic director of Salviati, British glass designer Simon Moore has endeavoured to bring this traditional glass-manufacturing company into the twenty-first century. The designs of Muehling, Grawunder and Maurer join those of Nigel Coates, Tom Dixon, Toord Boontje and Anish Kapoor, whose 1999 collection began to challenge the concepts of Venetian glassblowing and to lead it in new directions.

LEFT
Ingo Maurer
Vase, Blushing
Transparent, pierced glass
h. 50cm (19¾in) di. 23cm (9in)
Salviati, Italy

RIGHT
Ingo Maurer
Vase, I am a Vase
Transparent, pierced glass
h. 80cm (31¼in) di. 23cm (9in)
Salviati, Italy

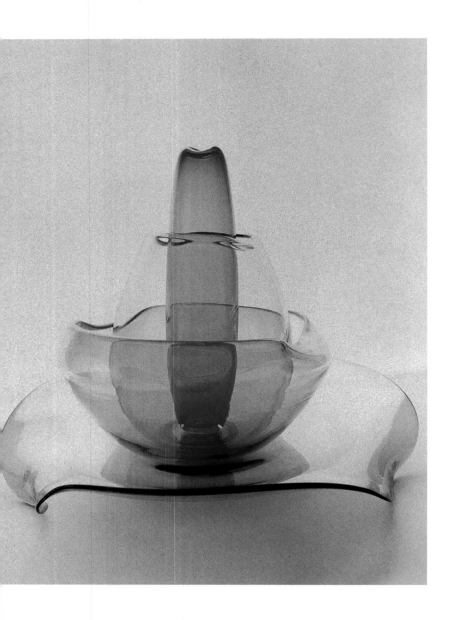

Ted Muehling
Centrepiece, Lotus
Hand blown glass
h. 50cm (19¹/₄in) di. 55cm (21¹/₄in)
Salviati, Italy
Limited batch production

Johanna Grawunder
Vase, Medusa
Hand modelled, blown transparent glass
w. 35cm (13⁵/₈in) h. 25cm (9³/₄in)
Salviati, Italy

Emmanuel Babled has long entertained the idea of inviting designers from different disciplines to experiment with the traditional art of Murano glass-blowing. Covo, which has a reputation for high-level craftsmanship, has given him the opportunity. As art director of the new 'Smash' collection he invited Jeffrey Bernet, Stephen Burks, Stefano Giovannoni, Richard Hutten, James Irvine, Ritsue Mishima, Marre Moerel and Jerszy Seymour to produce designs that were then given form by a master Murano blower. The results mix tradition and modernity in a series of impressive and poetic pieces. Through the use of designers from other fields, new challenges have been imposed on glass, with the process of the blowing often adding to the end result. Many of the designers, especially those more used to industrial processes, were often surprised at the unpredictability of the material. At the same time, however, they found that this element of serendipity in fact enhanced the final form. James Irvine commented: 'Like a typical industrial designer, I wanted to control the glass and design precise forms with precise shapes. But glass just doesn't work like that, so the surprise of the randomness of each form in fact became a pleasure for me. Every single one is slightly different.'

James Irvine
Cylinders
Glass
h. 38–40cm (14⁷⁄₈–15⁵⁄₈in)
di. 10cm (4in)
Covo srl, Italy

Jerszy Seymour
Vases, Ken Kuts
Glass
h. 16–30cm (6¹⁄₄–11⁷⁄₈in)
di. 13–17.5cm (5¹⁄₈–6⁷⁄₈in)
Covo srl, Italy

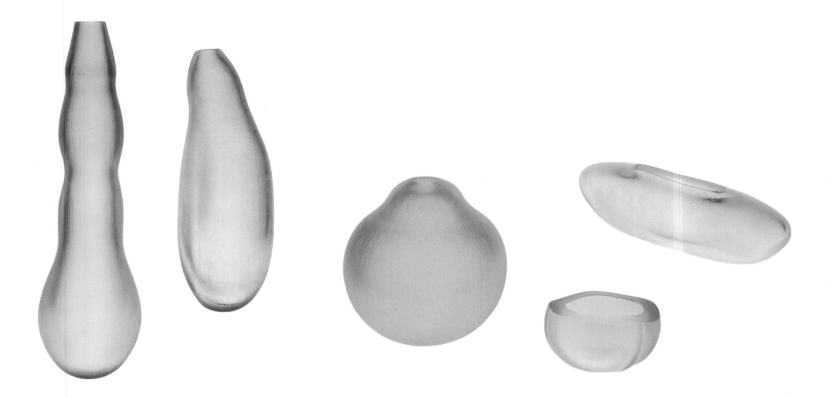

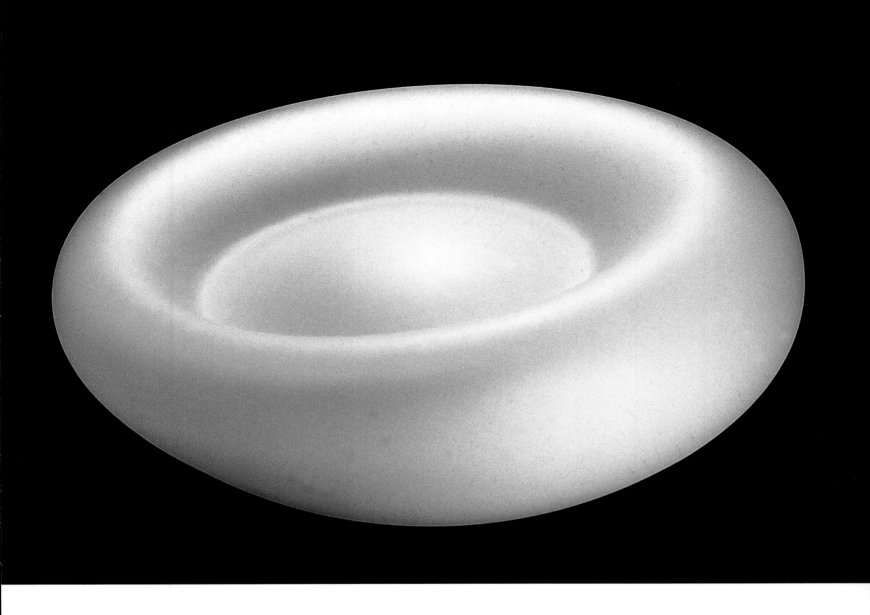

Ritsue Mishima
Vases, Serie Vegetali
Glass
h. 8–48cm (3 1/8–18 3/4 in)
di. 10–20cm (4–8in)
Covo srl, Italy

Lotte Thorsoe
Plate
Blown glass, free formed
h. 12cm (4 5/8 in) di. 38cm (14 7/8 in)
One-off

Olgoj Chorchoj
Vases, Twin Wall
Simax (heat resistant glass)
Various sizes
Libera, Czech Republic
Limited batch production

Isabel Hamm
Vase, Fish
Hand blown glass
h. 44cm (17^1/$_8$in) w. 13cm (5^1/$_8$in)
Isabel Hamm Glas, Germany
Limited batch production

Jacob de Baan was commissioned by the Netherlands Ministry of Economic Affairs' Ecological Department, in cooperation with Philips, Osram and Sylvania-Luminance, to develop an energy-saving lamp that would appeal to our aesthetic sensibilities and alter the ambience of a room rather than merely performing the function of lighting it economically. Working with Martijn Wegman, Marije Franssen and Angela van Woerdan, De Baan created 'Lamps of Desire', a collection comprising four solutions to

the project: 'Fruit', 'Glass', 'Twins' and 'Click'.

Far removed from the traditional and unimaginative designs normally associated with fluorescent bulbs, the prototypes are innovative, attractive and desirable objects in their own right; when I first saw examples of the 'Glass' concept in Milan, I thought they were perfume bottles. 'Click' is a mass-market product in which the light source already has the shape of a lamp and can be used directly either freestanding or free-hanging.

The lamp gives a sparkling warm red light reminiscent of the soft glow of a candle. The E-27 screw fitting is placed internally, and the lamp can be put into any normal E-27 fitting. The lamp has three 'clicking spots' on the outside, to which elements such as shades in various coloured plastics or metals can be easily attached. The 'Twins' concept is a family of lamps with the same shape but in different sizes and performing different functions – spotlight, reading lamp and so on. They are made in porcelain but finished in different

textures, and are sold in a combination with a remote control to create a variety of different effects from moonlit evening in Rio to Caribbean sunset. De Baan's fascination with the functioning of the human eye, his obsession with light and his desire to engage the emotions of the consumer, coupled with his technical expertise, have resulted in a new typology of energy-saving lamp – one that cannot only perform an environmentally-friendly job, but looks good too.

ABOVE
Jacob de Baan
Energy saving light, Fruit
Glass, steel and fluorescent technology
h. 11.5cm (4^1/$_2$in) di. 7.2cm (2^7/$_8$in)
Prototype

RIGHT
Jacob de Baan
Suspension light, Loom
Anodized, polished and/or painted aluminium
50w–200v hi spot
Small: h. 10.5cm (4^1/$_8$in)
di. 10cm (4in)
Large: h. 30cm (11^7/$_8$in)
di. 32.5cm (12^3/$_4$in)
Prototype

LEFT
Michele De Lucchi
Vase, Hermosa
Hand blown Murano glass
h. 30cm (11⅞in) di. 18cm (7in)
Produzione Privata, Italy
Limited batch production

RIGHT
Michele De Lucchi
Vase, Hansa
Hand blown Murano glass
h. 26cm (10⅛in) di. 18cm (7in)
Produzione Privata, Italy
Limited batch production

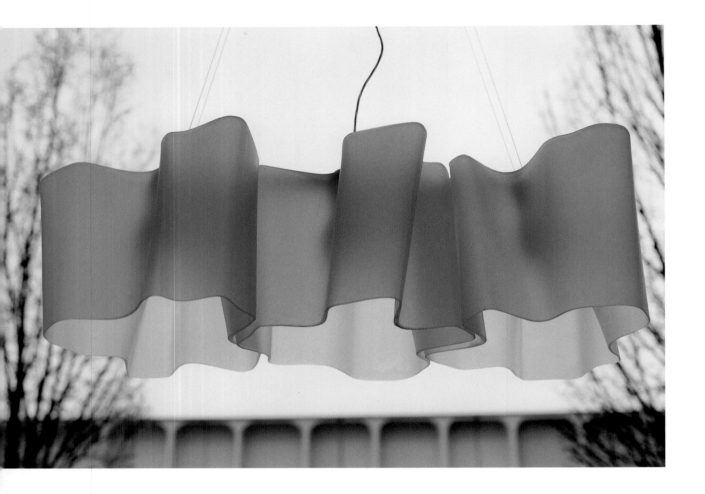

Michele De Lucchi and Gerhard Reichert
Suspension lamp, Logico System
Painted metal, blown glass opal diffuser
Each element: h. 63cm (24$^7/_8$in)
w. 68cm (26$^3/_4$in) l. 68cm (26$^3/_4$in)
150w (E27) A65
Artemide SpA, Italy

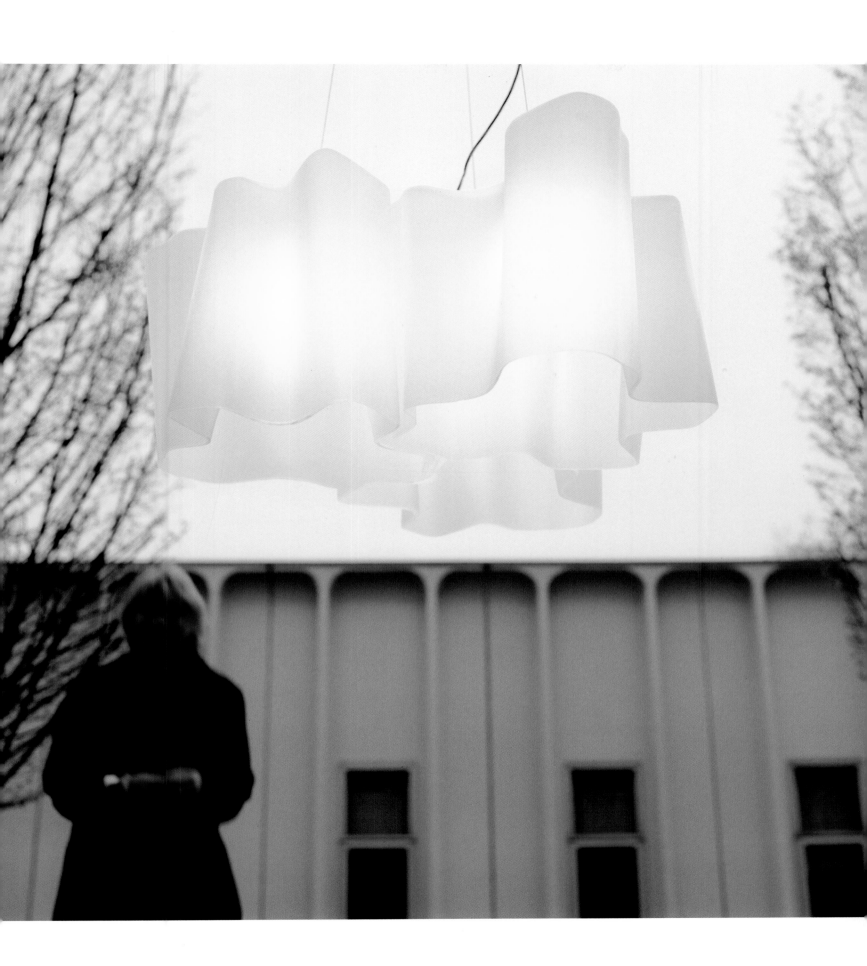

TEXTILES

Today we are seeing the emergence of some wonderful and increasingly sophisticated textiles, of which Sam Hecht's beautiful 'Fabrications' is an outstanding example. The weaving of textiles began, of course, with organic materials, but today there is an expanding use of non-organic, artificial materials or combinations – from carbon composites to polyamides – that have substantially progressed our creative potential. So far this has

occurred only in quite specialized fields, but if a broader perspective is taken towards the value of cultivating grasses or plants through genetic engineering in combination with polymers and resins so as to create new physical characteristics, it is an area that could advance on many planes. Perhaps, too, the industrial objects that we have grown accustomed to seeing as perfect and polished could become more earthy and tactile,

and in so doing produce a radical change in our value system.

Textiles have some unique characteristics – their micro-engineering allows the creation of both flexible clothes that breathe, expand and protect as well as the construction of lightweight, high-stress structures such as yachts and aerospace vehicles. In their ability to break free from formal constraints, I believe that textiles offer the

most logical and natural future of all material categories for the creation of new structures because of their remarkable flexibility in terms of scale and dimension. One important direction – shown here in several examples designed for the domestic context – is the printing or generation of textiles using a material such as glass so that they are able to carry light or current in a very three-dimensional way. It seems likely that such

innovations will once again pollinate other areas, from transportation to the built environment. Ultimately, textile design is the sphere in which all materials can converge with economy and purpose, whether for purely industrial reasons or for the beautification of our everyday lives through colour and composition.

Catellani & Smith
Light, Fil de fer
Pre-moulded aluminium
di: 10/60/90/120cm
(4/23⅝/35⅛/47¼in)
12v double ended halogen
Catellani & Smith, Italy

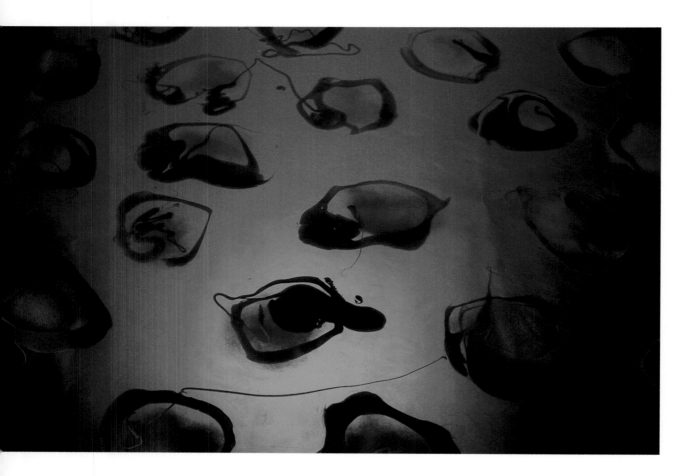

Harry & Camila
Textile, Underwater World
Cotton, rubber silicone
l. 100cm (39in) w. 135cm (52⁵/₈in)
Limited batch production

Hans Heisz
Suspension/floor lamp, Illustri
Steel, nomex
di. 35cm (13¾in)
Floor lamp: h. 185cm (72⁷/₈in)
1x60w bulb
Anthologie Quartett, Germany

OVERLEAF
Ronan and Erwan Bouroullec
Bookshelf, Brick
Polystyrene
h. 50cm (19½in) w. 300cm (117in)
d. 35cm (13¾in)
Cappellini SpA, Italy
Prototype

Floyd Paxton
Pendant light, Zoom
Flexible spring band steel, translucent
fabric sheeting
20 10W low voltage tungsten halogen
lamps
di. 20–130cm (7⁷/₈–51¹/₄in)
Serien GmbH, Germany

Yoshiki Hishinuma
Textile, polyurethane coated, synthetic
leather crepe
100% nylon tricot
Hishinuma Associates, Japan

OVERLEAF
Yoshiki Hishinuma
Polyurethane laminated and sheer dyed
crepe
100% polyester
Hishinuma Associates, Japan

Yoshiki Hishinuma began his career as one of Issey Miyake's assistants, travelling extensively to research new, exotic fabrics and then returning to experiment with ideas on how to translate these materials into fashion items. He expressed his opinions and ideas so freely that eventually a confrontation with Miyake resulted in his dismissal. Since then he has not collaborated with anyone and works with only the most progressive Japanese manufacturers, using modern artificial materials and the most up-to-date machinery. In his oeuvre textile design meets fashion and theatre. His clothes are body-conscious and are distinctive in their form and construction, in which haute couture and handicraft are combined. He became famous in the 1980s for his huge kitelike items of clothing,

which relied on wind to give them their final form, and over the years his personal approach to fabrics has resulted in highly dynamic and individual collections of textiles that are then transformed into structural, organic and colourful creations for the catwalk. He frequently uses traditional methods of tie-dying and smocking, yet reinterprets these by the addition of hi-tech materials or industrial processes. Interesting developments are the use of matt coloured polyurethane paper bonded by heat to woven polyester or knitted-cotton textiles; the application of collage consisting of woollen fabrics and knitwear; the use of bright opaque lacquered colours over thin supple art fibre; heat-cutting polyester film tape; and the manufacture of metallic denim clothes. His own

experimentation remains the core of his collections: 'I'm not interested in fashion trends. Concepts come from personal thought.' He has an inquisitive mind that continually looks at fabrics to liberate their inherent potential. For example, having reflected on what would happen if he boiled a sheepskin rug, he proceeded to apply the same process to a range of materials that ultimately gave rise to his shrink collections of the mid-1990s. At the same time he created his own primitive felt by repeatedly boiling and treading natural yarns. He then discovered a yarn that had the unique property of shrinking but which remained in its natural state if pre-heat-treated. Hishinuma exploited this discovery to create a series of fabrics of varying surface textures.

The designer's enquiring mind is not only directed towards the materials themselves but also towards new ways of achieving surprising colour effects. For many years Hishinuma worked with an engineer to develop a process whereby he could dye only those parts of a fabric he wanted to colour. This led to the development of a 'wonder dye' that stains material simply by dabbing. His 2001 collection again works with burnt, boiled or laminated polyester, which this year has been coated with polyurethane and laser-cut to produce synthetic leather and fascinating textures. 'It's important for the first concept to grow and change freely,' he writes, 'I am not a conceptual artist; the concept is only the starting point.'

Alberto Meda
Chair, Rolling Frame Desk Chair
Die-cast aluminium, PVC covered
polyester mesh
h. 99cm (39in) w. 43cm (17in)
d. 75cm (29½in)
Alias SpA, Italy

The 'Rolling Frame Chair' by
Alberto Meda offers both elegance
and practicality for the domestic
office. In this addition to the now
famous series, Meda has combined an extruded aluminium
frame with a PVC-covered polyester mesh seat. The profile is
light and delicate – attributes
that, combined with the transparency of the PVC, make the
chair as suitable for the dinner
table as for the desk.

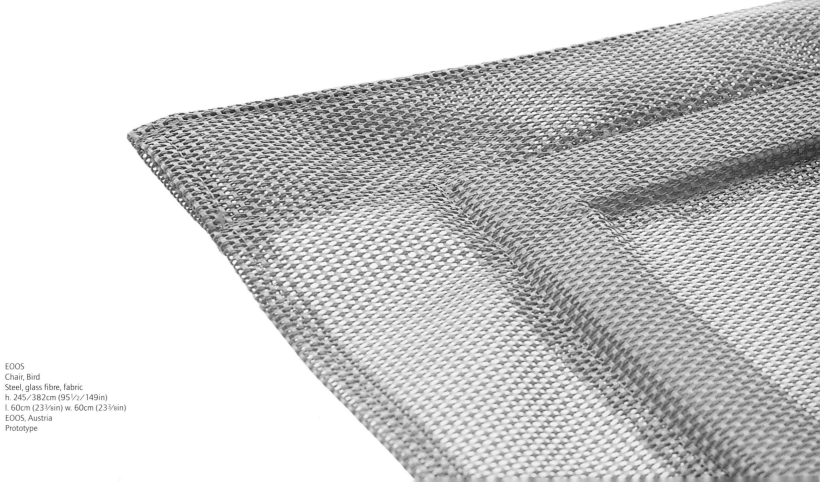

EOOS
Chair, Bird
Steel, glass fibre, fabric
h. 245/382cm (95½/149in)
l. 60cm (23⅜in) w. 60cm (23⅜in)
EOOS, Austria
Prototype

Sam Hecht/Ideo
Communication tools, Fabrications
Elektex cloth, polyurethane and
methacrylate
Soft remote: h. 8cm (3¹⁄₈in)
w. 6.2cm (2³⁄₈in) l. 14cm(5¹⁄₂in)
Soft keyboard: h. 2.8cm (1⁷⁄₈in)
w. 30.2cm (11⁷⁄₈in) l. 14cm (5¹⁄₂in)
Electrotextiles, UK

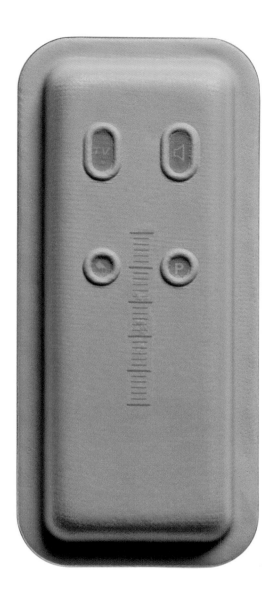

Eric Gizard
Carpet
100% polyamide solution dyed yarn,
Chromatonic printing system
l. 50cm (19^1/$_2$in) w. 50cm (19^1/$_2$in)
Tarkett Sommer, France

No Picnic
Seat/Frame, Ram
Elastic lycra, enamelled steel frame,
leather seat
h. 159cm (62in) l. 106cm (41^3/$_8$in)
d. 84cm (32^3/$_4$in)
Felicerossi, Italy

TOP LEFT
Harry & Camila
Textile, Dried flowers
Natural dried flowers, transparent fabric,
rubber silicone
l. 135cm (52⅝in) w. 200cm (78in)
Limited batch production

BOTTOM LEFT
Harry & Camila
Textile, Dried flowers pillow
Natural dried flowers, transparent fabric,
rubber silicone
l. 40/50/60cm
(15⅝/19½/23⅜in)
w. 40/50/60cm
(15⅝/19½/23⅜in)
Limited batch production

Claudy Jongstra
Ermine Bedcover
Merino wool, cashmere, silk chiffon
l. 200cm (78in) w. 220cm (85⅞in)
Not tom dick & harry, the Netherlands

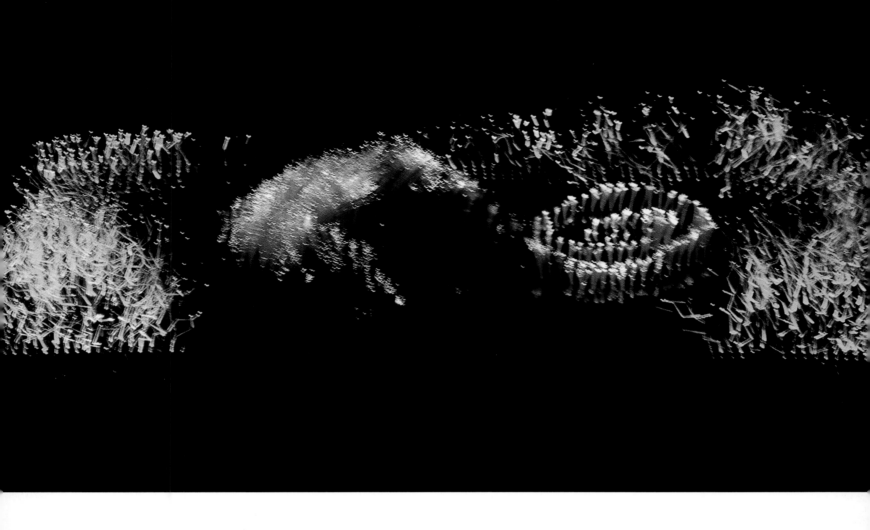

Sarah Taylor
Interactive sensory panel, Interactive
Fibre Optic Panel
Polymer Optical Fibres
h. 120cm (46⅞in) w. 80cm (31¼in)
l. 105cm (41in)
Sarah Taylor Design, UK
Limited batch production

Textile design becomes installation
art. In collaboration with the
University of York, British designer
Sarah Taylor designed her interactive panel for the multi-sensory
exhibition 'Coming to our Senses'.
By stimulating bunches of fibre
optics, weird and wonderful sound
and lighting effects are produced.

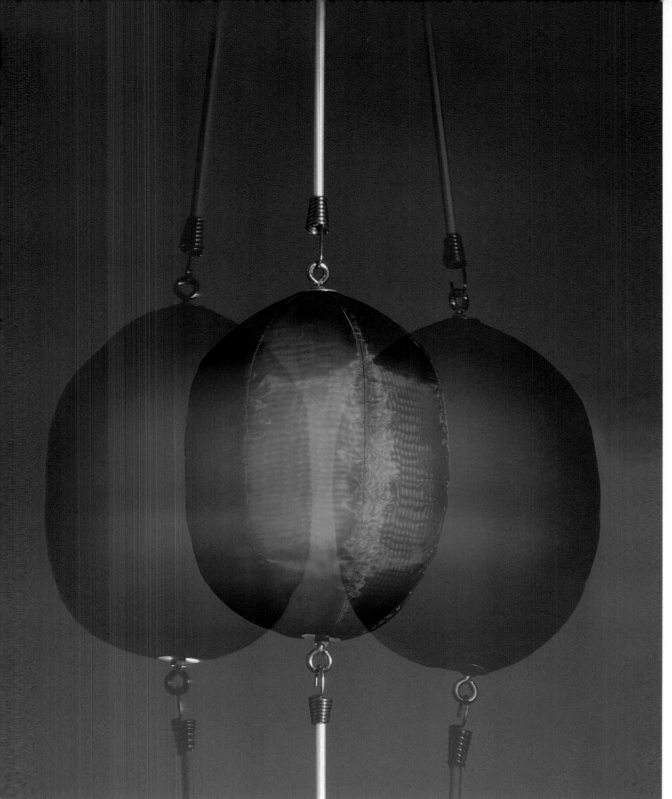

LEFT
Stiletto Design/Nexus Design
Pendant light, Light Club
Red LEDs, 6V battery, expansion rubber
band
h. 27cm (10⁵/₈in) di. 20cm (7⁷/₈in)
Stiletto Design Vertreib, Germany

FACING
Stiletto Design/Nexus Design
Pillow Light
Soft hemp fabric, red LEDs, 6v battery
l. 35cm (13⁵/₈in) w. 35cm (13⁵/₈in)
Stiletto Design Vertreib, Germany

Additions to Stiletto's series of
playful lighting objects, 'Pillow
Light' and 'Light Club' have been
designed to be both caressed and
abused. They can be held, thrown,
kicked or punched – without sus-
taining damage. The LEDs are
activated by touch and extinguish
after twenty minutes.

Laurene Leon Boym
Rug, Glow
Wool, phosphorescent yarn
w. 183cm (72in) l. 183cm (72in)
Handy, USA
Limited batch production

Gruppe RE
Illuminating glass tile, Onda
Glass, glass enamels, luminating
pigment
Each tile l. 17cm (6⁵/₈in) w. 30cm
(11³/₄in)
Prototype

Gruppe RE
Illuminating wallpaper, Linea, Corso
Paper, screenprinting colours,
luminating pigment
l. 212cm (82⁵/₈in) w. 256cm (99⁷/₈in)
Prototype

Unbeknownst to each other and working on different sides of the Atlantic, US designer Laurene Leon Boym and the German design team Gruppe RE have simultaneously been experimenting with the use of phosphorescence, adding glow-in-the dark pigments to everyday design staples. Boym uses a specially created yarn to outline the shape of the pattern in her rugs, while Gruppe RE's wallpapers and glass tiles become three-dimensional once the lights are switched off.

Gruppe RE, founded by Nicole Hüttner and Silke Warchold, launched these intriguing products at the 'Nachtschwarmer' during Passagen 2001 in Cologne. Along with three other female designers they created a series of objects that react chameleon-like to changes in lighting conditions: 'In our work there is mainly one theme we are interested in: to treat materials and surfaces in a special way and to show a new value within the design.'

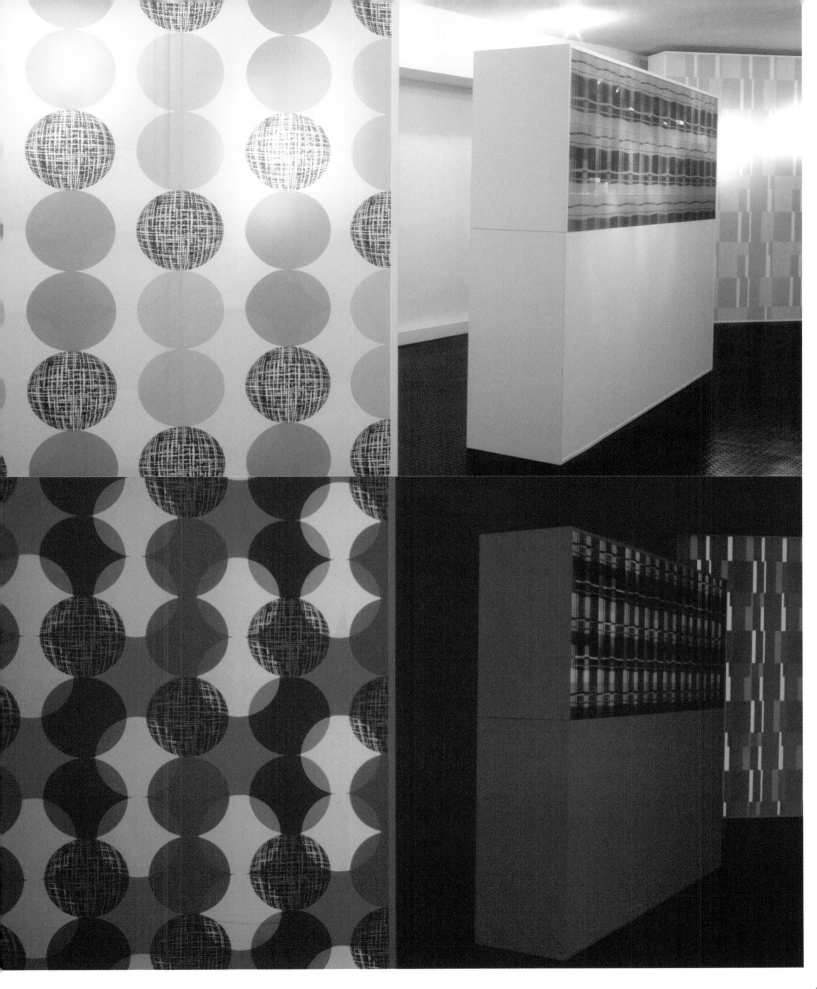

LEFT
Carol Westfall
Textile, Humanity
Digital print on cotton
h. 149.8cm (59in) w. 97.8cm (38½in)
One-off

FACING
Carol Westfall
Textile, Portobello Shoes
Digital print on cotton
h. 149.8cm (59in) w. 97.8cm (38½in)
One-off

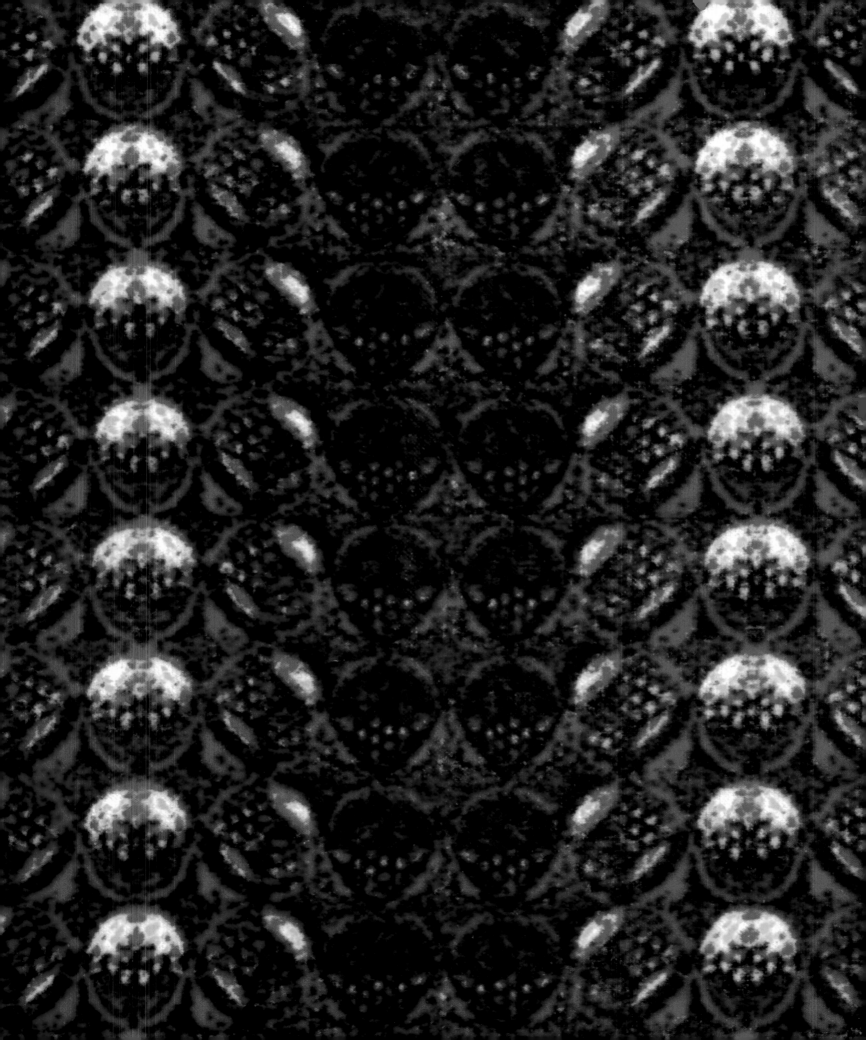

Debbie Jane Buchan
Silkscreen printed fabric, Untitled
Cotton velvet
w. 118cm (46¼in) l. 320cm (124⅞in)
One-off

Flavia Alves de Souza
Lounger, Pororoga
Stainless steel, translucent∕fluorescent
plastic film
h. 77cm (30in) l. 120cm (46⅞in)
w. 51cm (20in)
Edra SpA, Italy

Edra's 2001 collection was conceived as the furniture equivalent of haute couture. Massimo Morozzi, Edra's artistic director, readily admits that the collection is for the luxury market but that what really matters to him 'is the emotional and spiritual sense of the product, the sensuous luxury of using it.' In the collection, drama and colour are used to compensate for the emotional poverty of minimalist design. 'It is a collection that has rediscovered the pleasure of daring', Morozzi comments. Certainly, the sheer pinkness and scale of the pieces shock at every turn.

The Campana brothers have produced large disc screens/windbreaks with frames of stainless steel crisscrossed by a web of transparent and coloured plastic tubing. They have used the same materials in their chair 'Anemone', which looks as if it were designed in the 1960s for the sci-fi film *Barbarella*.

Fernando and Humberto Campana
Armchair, Anemone
Stainless steel, plastic tubing
h. 70cm (27⁵/₈in) w. 100cm (43³/₈in)
d. 80cm (31¹/₂in)
Edra SpA, Italy

Debbie Jane Buchan
Textile and fashion fabric design,
Multi Blooms
Screen shot
Prototype

Claudy Jongstra
Bedcover, Sunflower
Merino wool, Gotland Pels, raw silk, silk
changeant organza
l. 350cm (136½in) w. 220cm (85⅞in)
Not tom, dick & harry, the Netherlands

OVERLEAF
Harry & Camila
Textile, Tessuto Marina
Seaweed, stuffing textile, rubber silicone
l. 135cm (52⅝in) w. 200cm (78in)

Claudy Jongstra
Carpet, Drenthe Heath
Merino wool, Drenthe Heath, cotton
l. 300cm (117in) w. 110cm (42⅞in)
Not tom, dick & harry, the Netherlands   119

Avec Group/Ivan Baj
Carpet cushion covers
100% handspun merino wool
Arcade Group, Italy

Produced by Arcade, 'Avec' is a
home and textile collection hand-
made in Brazil by an indigenous
workforce. Not only are all the
pieces ecologically friendly, using
only the most natural dyes and
pure fibres, but the main aim
of 'Avec' is to promote a native
community. All the work is carried
out in private homes, and traditional
weaving patterns and materials
have been rescued from oblivion.
The contemporary designs of Ivan
Baj, however, bring a centuries-old
industry into the new millennium.

Danskina
Carpet, Corale
100% pure new wool
Danskina, the Netherlands

Eric Robin
Vase, Marlene
Ceramic, fur
h. 50cm (19½in) di. 20cm (7⅞in)
Eric Robin Design, France
Limited batch production

Claudy Jongstra
Wall Hanging, Red Ribbon
Merino wool, raw silk, silk organza
l. 350cm (136½in) w. 120cm (46⅞in)
Not tom, dick & harrry, the Netherlands

Eric DeWitt
Chair, Coathanger Furniture
PVC pipe, upholstered dots, stainless
steel rod, hardware
h. 91.4cm (36in) w. 66cm (26in)
d. 61cm (24in)
Prototype

Vibeke Rohland
Textile print, Pills Stills
Flax, reactive colour, silkscreen
h. 70cm (27⅜in) l. 80cm (31¼in)
One-off

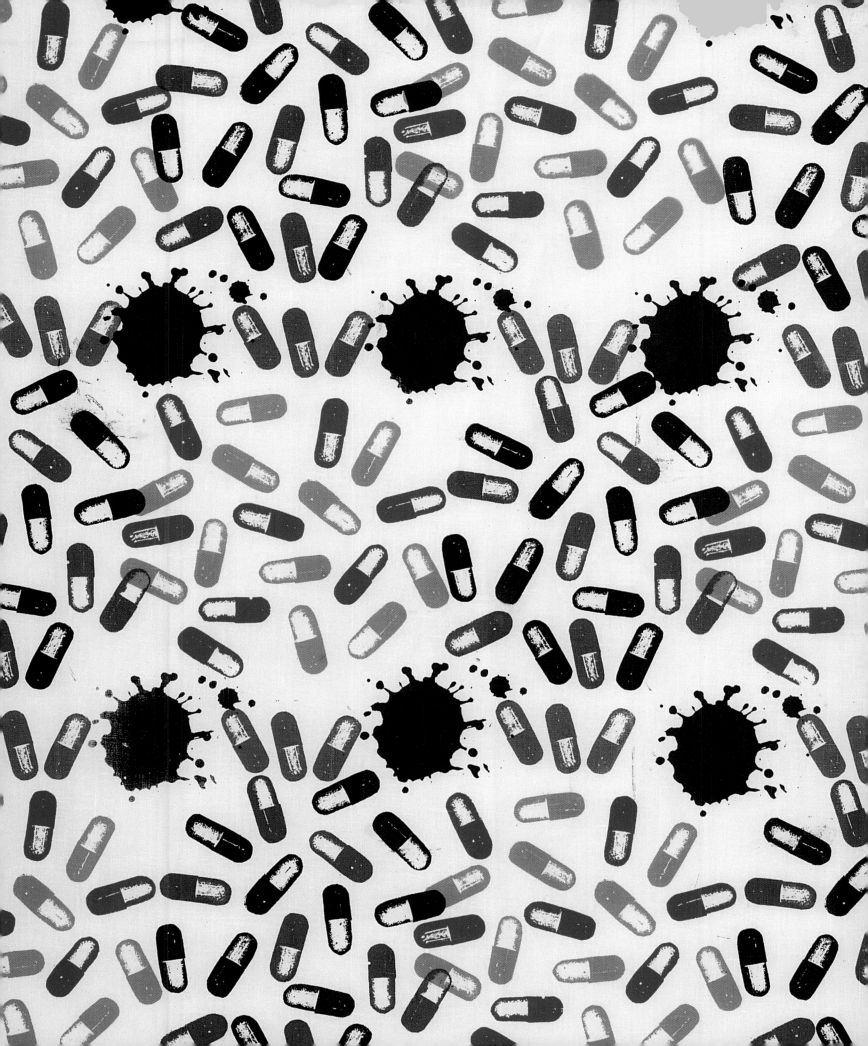

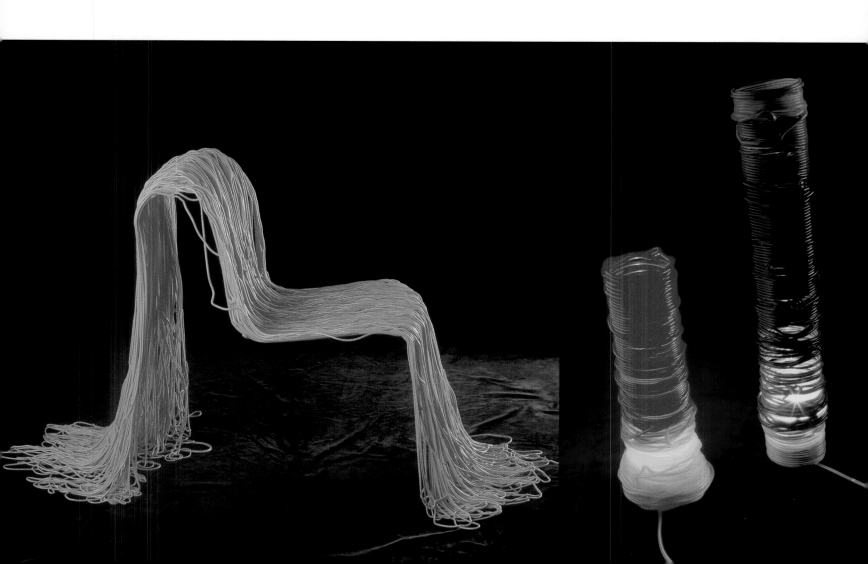

FACING, TOP
Christian Ghion
Carpet tiles, Anticipations
100% polyamide
w. 50cm (19½in) l. 50cm (19½in)
Tarkett Sommer, France

FACING, BOTTOM LEFT
Karim Rashid
Chair, Pink Bubble Chair
Extruded plastic
One-off

FACING, BOTTOM RIGHT
Michele De Lucchi
Lamp, Designer Lamps
Extruded plastic
One-off

ABOVE
Karim Rashid
Upholstered sofa, Momo Pink 100
Steel frame, upholstery
l. 7.6m (299in) h. 304cm (120in)
d. 457cm (180in)
One-off installation

More art installation than furniture,
this 7.6-metre-wide sofa was first
shown at the New York art gallery
Deitch Projects. 'Momo Pink 100'
consists of forty-three pieces and
can seat up to a hundred people.
In the future he hopes to substitute
the pink fabric with Smartwear
so that the user can audio-video
telecommunicate while relaxing.

Yoshiki Hishinuma
Transfer printed rib stitch
100% polyester
Hishinuma Associates, Japan

Claudio Colucci
Carpet Tile
100% polyamide solution dyed yarn,
chromatonic printing system
l. 50cm (19¾in) w. 50 cm (19¾in)
Tarkett Sommer, France

Charles and Ray Eames
Large and Small Dot Fabric
Cotton, polyester, Teflon®
w. 142.2cm (56in)
Maharam, USA

Verner Panton
Textile, Geometri
Cotton, polyester, Teflon® finish
w. 139.7cm (55in)
132   Maharam, USA

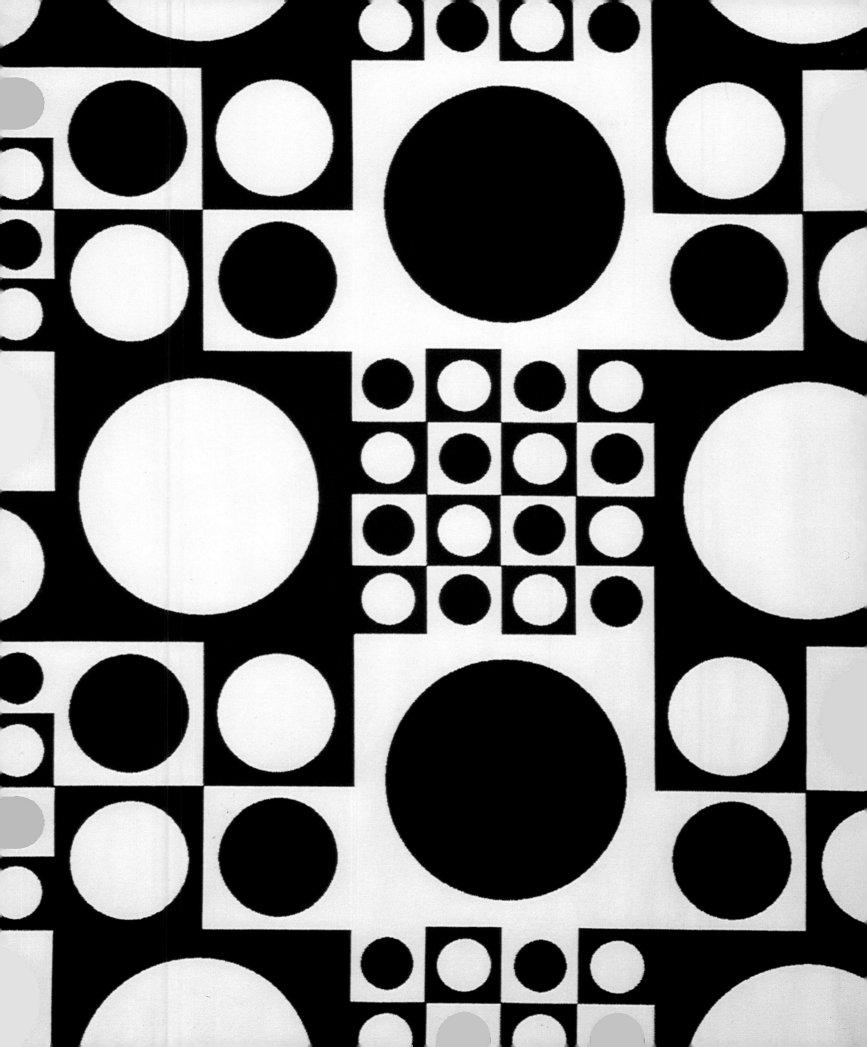

Alexander Girard
Textiles, Facets, Double Triangle, Checker
Cotton, polyester, Teflon® finish
w. 139.7cm (55in)
Maharam, USA

Fabio Novembre
Rug, Net
Polypropylene rope, stainless steel discs
Large: l. 600cm (234in) w. 200cm (78in)
Medium: l. 450cm (175½in) w. 200cm
(78in)
Small: l. 300cm (117in) w. 150cm
(58 ½in)
Cappellini SpA, Italy

OVERLEAF
Patrick Norguet
Armchair and two seater sofa,
Rive Droite
Plywood, polyurethane steel,
Pucci fabric
Armchair: h. 69cm (26⅞in)
w. 98cm (38¼in) d. 76cm (29⅝in)
Sofa: h. 69cm (26⅞in) l. 180cm
(70¼in) d. 76cm (29⅝in)
Cappellini SpA, Italy

WOOD

Despite the limited title, this section contains a wealth of objects made in wood, paper, cork, even rubber. During a recent trip to Amsterdam I was taken to see a modern jewellery shop called Ra. There I found some paper pieces by the designer Nel Linssen that literally took my breath away. They were simultaneously both primitive and modern, combining a basic material with a superlative degree of constructional innovation. Paradoxically, this new world of design that revisits the non-technological is often itself highly technological – so that, for example, the cardboard tubes used by Shigeru Ban for the Japanese pavilion at the Hanover Expo were in fact made in a highly industrialized way. In terms of surface properties, plywood comes closest to paper and has proved itself of enduring utility. In its extreme mouldability – a somewhat unpredictable property that can be achieved only through the physics of manufacture – Jakob Gebert's new 'Taino' chair for Vitra redefines the plastic potential of this remarkable material.

This section has perhaps the highest concentration of experimental objects in the *Yearbook*. Together they categorically prove that from Zumtor to Ban, from De Lucchi to Piano, and from Loom to Inform to Vitra some of the most influential thinkers and manufacturers of today continue to see great cultural relevance in pushing the structural and poetic limits of these humanist materials.

Barber Osgerby Associates
Table, Shell
Curved plywood
h. 73cm (28½in)
w. 140/180cm (54⅝/70¼in)
l. 140/190cm (54⅝/74⅛in)
Cappellini SpA, Italy

Jakob Gebert
Stacking chair, Taino
Wood, aluminium
h. 82cm (32in) w. 49cm (19⅛in)
d. 56cm (21⅞in)
Vitra AG, Switzerland

Jakob Gebert, collaborating with Vitra, has produced a chair using two pressed-wood shells of fine layers each sandwiched around the chair legs rather than the typical two-layer shell mounted on top of the legs. 'Because it is a single unit,' he says, 'it is a stronger chair. It's funny, but I found that the connection between wood and metal is better than that between wood and wood.'

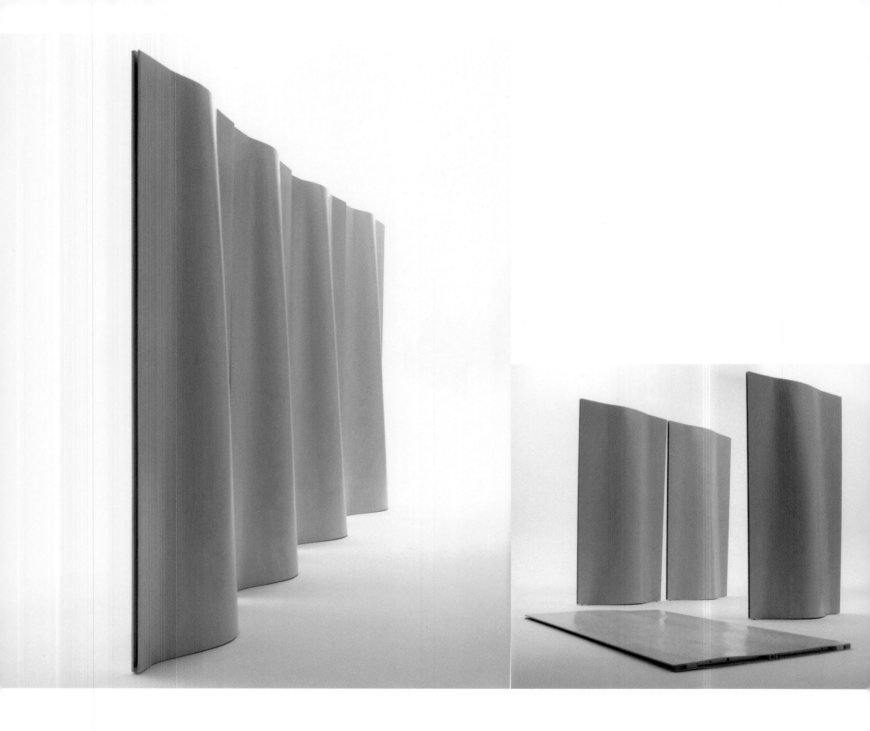

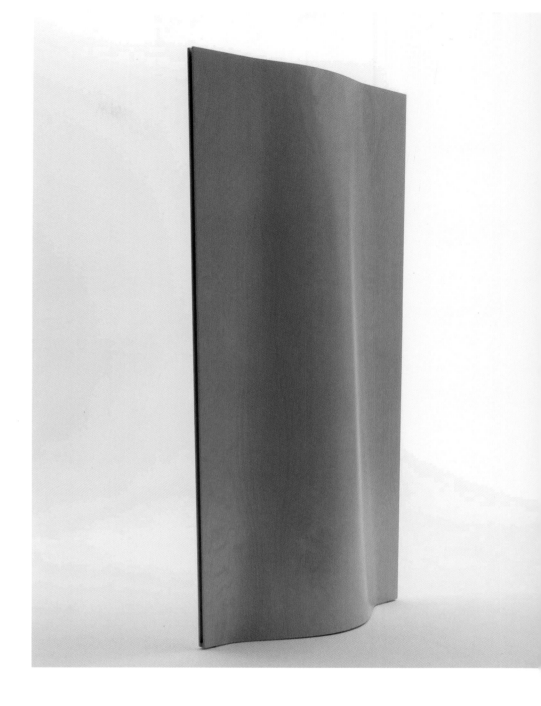

Paolo Ulian
Screen, UP
Coverflex plywood
h. 170cm (67in) w. 35cm (13³⁄₄in)
l. 100 cm (39³⁄₈in)
BBB Bonacina, Italy

Thanks to the countless reinter-
pretations of the straight-backed
minimalist chair, plywood is probably the most undervalued material
on the market today. Yet handled
intelligently, its simple, pared-down
aesthetic allows the contemporary
designer to exhibit his or her skill,
the repeated folding of very thin
sheets providing an opportunity
to offer a delicate profile while
retaining the almost incredible
weight-bearing properties.

Paolo Ulian's screen is the result
of his discovery of Coverflex – an
extraordinarily flexible plywood
3.5 millimetres thick that was
patented in Italy two years ago by
the Jolando Eliseo Molteni company. The screen is sold flat-packed,
but with a simple action – the
pushing in of the vertical sides – it
transforms into a three-dimensional
object that can just as easily be
restored to its flat form for transportation. The screen is soft, elastic
and very light, weighing just 10
kilograms, but has a solid, almost
monolithic, presence once opened.

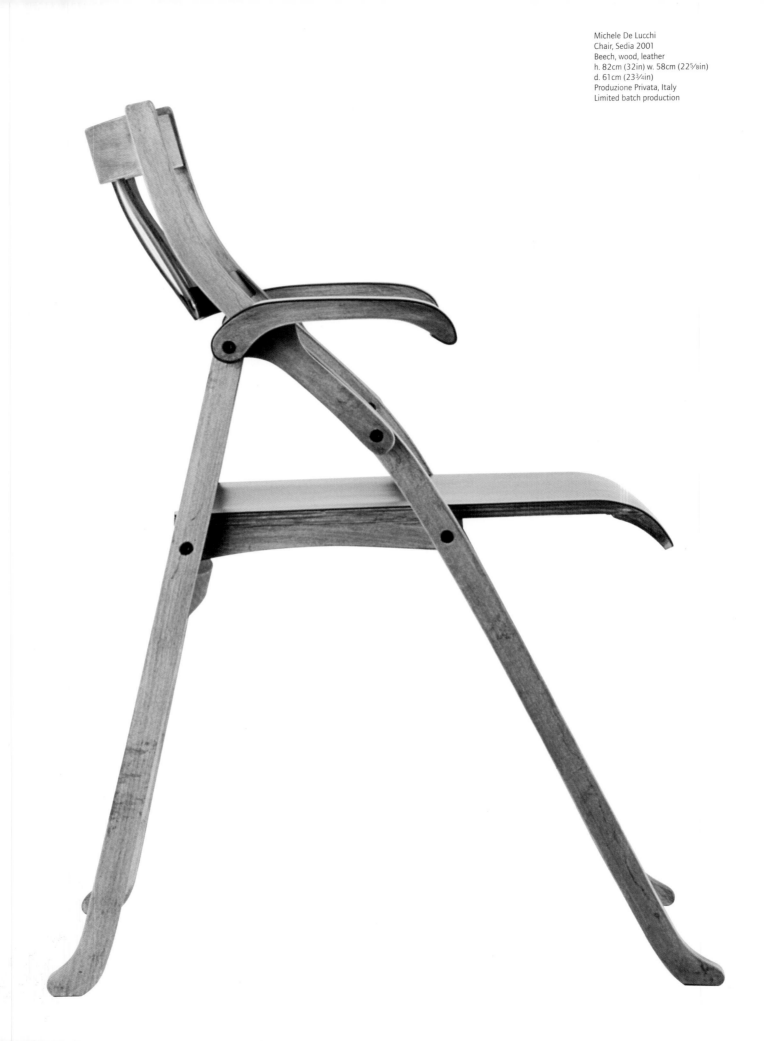

Michele De Lucchi
Chair, Sedia 2001
Beech, wood, leather
h. 82cm (32in) w. 58cm (22⅝in)
d. 61cm (23¾in)
Produzione Privata, Italy
Limited batch production

Michael Toepffer
Wardrobe, Trunk
Polyester, wood
h. 196cm (77¼in) w. 94cm (37in)
d. 63cm (24¾in)
One-off

Robert Wettstein
Chair, Bastian
Paper, wood
h. 80cm (31¼in) w. 44cm (17⅛in)
l. 121cm (47⅝in)
Structure Design, Switzerland

147

Richard Hutten
Paper money bowl
250,000 Dutch guilder notes
h. 5cm (2in) di. 36cm (14in)
One-off

The homogenization of Europe
has some 'interesting' spin-offs.
Richard Hutten has used 250,000
of the last Dutch guilders to be
produced before the definitive
introduction of the Euro in 2002
to fabricate a bowl.

Markus Benesch
Cupboard, Yourside
Lacquered MDF, transparent acrylic glass
h. 180cm (73⁵⁄₈in) l. 130cm (50³⁄₄in)
d. 40cm (15⁵⁄₈in)
Money for Milan, Germany

Nel Linssen
Necklace
Reinforced, folded paper
One-off

Nike
Shoe, Air Woven
Hand woven static and elastic webbing,
phylon sole
Nike, USA
Limited edition

153

ABOVE
Kenneth Cobonpue
Chair and Ottoman, Balou
Abaca (Manila hemp) rattan vines,
metal, cotton
Chair: h. 75cm (29½in) w. 95cm
(37½in) d. 95cm (37½in)
Ottoman: h. 38cm (15in) w. 89cm
(35in) d. 61cm (24in)
Interior Crafts of the Islands Inc.,
the Philippines

LEFT
Betty Cobonpue, Kenneth Cobonpue
Armchair, Yin & Yang
Steel, rattan, rattan skin, wood
h. 71cm (28in) w. 90cm (35½in)
d. 76cm (29⁷∕₈in)
Interior Crafts of the Islands Inc.,
the Philippines

FACING
Kenneth Cobonpue
Armchair and sofa, Pigalle
Abaca (Manila hemp), nylon, steel
Chair: h. 79cm (31⅛in) w. 97cm
(38¼in) d. 94cm (37in)
Sofa: h. 75cm (29½in) w. 158cm
(62¼in) d. 100cm (39³∕₈in)
Interior Crafts of the Islands Inc.,
the Philippines

The last few years have seen a second wave of foreign influence hit the Italian market, after the the 1980s when there was an increase in collaboration between Italian companies and countries such as the Netherlands, Finland and Switzerland. The more recent contributions have come from countries such as Brazil, Israel, Portugal and the United States, which, if not directly working with Italian manufacturers, are now taking a much more active role in the international design scene. The innovative avant-garde styles of, for example, the Portuguese Voyager Group and the Brazilian

Campana brothers and Faz Group have now filtered through and are being taken up by Italian design businesses.

New this year are works by a Philippine group, Movement 8. Like Ross Lovegrove, Movement 8 has a profound respect for the natural world, from which they derive their organic and biomorphic forms. One of the group's members, Kenneth Cobonpue, describes his design philosophy as 'looking at nature with the purity and innocence of a child. There you find perfect visual qualities that are waiting to be transformed

into modern man-made objects.' The aim of the group is to bring their work into the global mainstream while retaining their own heritage, in which Malaysian, Spanish and Mexican influences are combined. They want to move the past into the present by seeing things with a fresh eye, using natural materials in unexpected and innovative ways and mixing traditional skills with modern technology. Most of the designs presented show a restraint of form and economy of embellishment that emphasize textural detail and surface pattern. They have a purity of form that is not the aesthetic

sterility of minimalism but rather a dematerialization, or honing-down, of the unnecessary in order to enhance the sensual and emotional impact of both the workmanship and the inherent quality of the simple materials used.

Lovegrove believes that 'the new epoch we are entering will be exciting because finally designers seen as pluralist or idiosyncratic, craft-based or low-tech, will begin to dominate the creative world by virtue of a completely free view of how materials and technology can be harmonized.'

TOP LEFT
Fernando and Humberto Campana
Bamboo chair
Bamboo, powdered steel
h. 100cm (39³⁄₈in) w. 42cm (16½in)
d. 53cm (20⁷⁄₈in)
Hidden, the Netherlands

BOTTOM LEFT
Fernando and Humberto Campana
Chair, Mixed Series
Bamboo, acrylic
h. 67cm (26³⁄₈in) w. 46cm (18⅛in)
d. 52cm (20½in)
Studio Campana, Brazil

ABOVE
Fernando and Humberto Campana
Cardboard sofa
Corrugated cardboard and metal
h. 80cm (31¼in) w. 180cm (70¼in)
l. 70cm (27³⁄₈in)
Edra SpA, Italy

It would be fair to say that Edra discovered the Campanas. In 1996 the company produced the brothers' 'Vermelha' knotted chair and put them well and truly on the international design map. Their designs mix native Brazilian low-tech craftsmanship and recycled or raw materials, but translate this seemingly humble combination into a formula suitable for Italian manufacturing. The brothers consider that the otherwise technically competent Brazilian furniture industry lacks daring and is divorced from the contemporary design market, and for this reason they currently prefer to collaborate with foreign companies. However, they believe that it won't be long before their own country comes to a fuller understanding of the cooperation required between designer, art director, technicians and production in order to create exciting modern design.

All the Campanas' furniture is characterized by a blend of the artisanal and the industrial. Much of their current work, for example, combines natural fibres, such as sisal, straw and rattan, with synthetic materials and surfaces. Their aim is to borrow techniques from the traditional crafts to make modern designs, or else to use simple folk materials in industrial processes. 'We are not interested in naive, romantic primitivism,' they claim, 'progress cannot be stopped. The problem is to coexist with the transformation without losing the knowledge contained in materials and techniques.'

The muted, straight-lined 'Humble' folded cardboard furniture range, comprising a table, screen and sofa, is inspired by the cardboard collected for recycling by the poor of São Paolo in Brazil. Each day's booty of boxes is folded into striking patterns and then pulled through the streets on handcarts to the paper plant. The Campanas have borrowed these quasi-poetic forms, dyeing the cardboard and adding metal mesh to give strength to the pieces. According to Stephen Hamel, PR head for Edra, they have taken 'the richness of the poor and made a luxury out of it'.

Marcel Wanders seems to be a man of contradictions. His dream is to 'select a great team and build the best office chair for Vitra', yet he is the creator of many inventive, playful and thought-provoking designs for Droog Design, including the well-known 'Fish Net Chair', first produced in 1996 which has now been given a metallic makeover by Cappellini. The year 2001 saw the foundation of Moooi, which, although owned and guided by Casper Vissers, is art-directed by Wanders. It includes the former 'Wanders Wonders' collection, and for now its output consists almost entirely

of his own work, although other designers are being invited to collaborate in the future. For Wanders, design is a process of learning; he is constantly questioning and creating new connections: 'No particular consideration in the concept of a design is greater than any other – not the material, technology, technique, function, price or meaning – it is the successful marrying of these aspects that creates a successful object. However, the only starting point for me is the individual for whom ... the design is intended.' Although Wanders does research and experiment with new materials and

technology, his main preoccupation is with the 'brains, habits, nature and the hearts of people'. He does not consider success and popularity to have changed his work at all. He sees little difference between his early work for Droog and the work done more recently for clients such as Rosenthal and British Airways. His success has, he says, 'changed only my possibilities, the size of my public and therefore my responsibilities'.

The vision behind the 'Airborn Snotty Vases' was to make the unseen seen. Wanders wanted to find a hi-tech way of creating a

series of objects inspired by existent yet non-visual shapes. An individual was invited to sneeze several times into a very powerful scanner capable of recording microscopic particles. The most 'beautiful' particle patterns were selected and transferred to a computer, where they were modified using specially created IFN software to form CAD images. The results were sent to an SLS machine, which, using 3-D drawing and a computer-guided laser, built up unique models. Let's just hope that Cappellini doesn't make us pay through the nose for these enchanting little pieces.

Marcel Wanders
Airborn Snotty Vases
Polyamide ore in non-pro terms nylon
h. 15cm (5⁷⁄₈in) w. 15cm (5⁷⁄₈in)
l. 15cm (5⁷⁄₈in)
Cappellini SpA, Italy

Michael Sodeau
Coat stand, Corallo
Cane
h. 190cm (74¹⁄₈in) di. 75cm (29¹⁄₄in)
Gervasoni, Italy

Kevin Walz
Floor/wall tile
100% natural cork
h. 30cm (11⁷⁄₈in) w. 90cm (35¹⁄₂in)
KorQinc, USA

Kevin Walz
Vase, The Big Vase
100% natural cork
h. 19cm (7³⁄₄in) di. 14.5cm (5⁵⁄₈in)
KorQinc, USA

The ProntoKorQ collection is
100 per cent environmentally friendly. Cork is the harvested bark of the
Quercus sughero – the Mediterranean
oak. The material used here is recycled from the bottle stopper industry
and has been compressed to the
greatest possible density. KorQinc
harnesses the natural properties of
the cork – resilience and responsive-
ness – and combines these with new
technologies to give the material
structural capabilities.

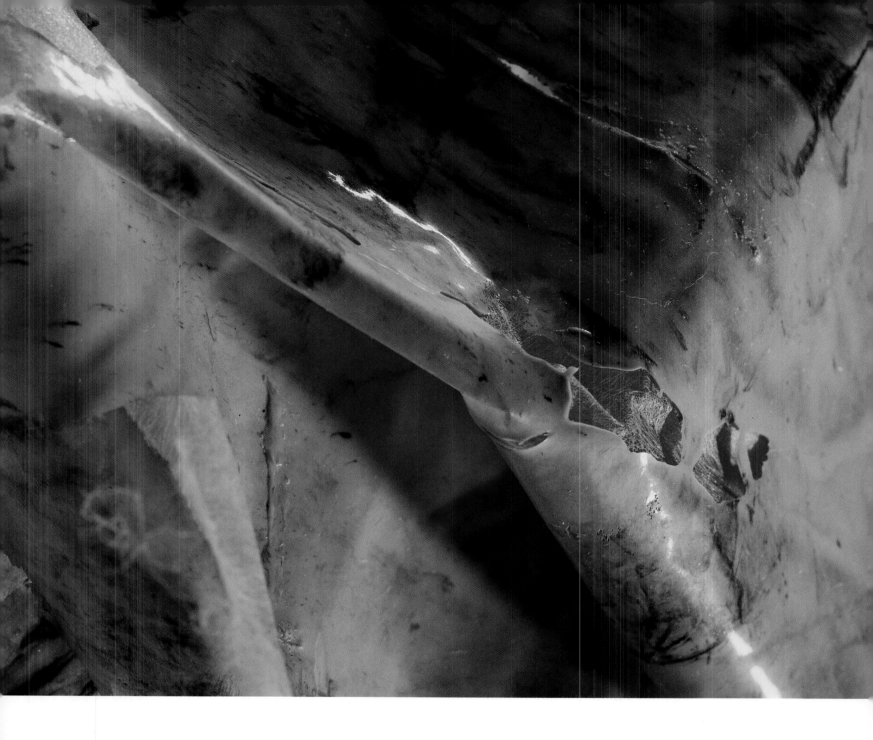

Fabio Carlesso
Textile, Wood Burri
Silicone and resin treated fabric
Blue Project Team, Italy

Komplot Design
Chair, Non
PUR-rubber
h. 76cm (30in) w. 44cm(17³⁄₈in)
d. 41cm (16¹⁄₈in)
Källemo AB, Sweden

The success of a design can lay in
the re-adaptive use of materials.
Komplot Design have used PUR-
rubber in their 'Non' chair. With
simple straight geometric lines
and integral spring bands for
comfort, the product is a piece of
non-design that is at home either
in or out of doors.

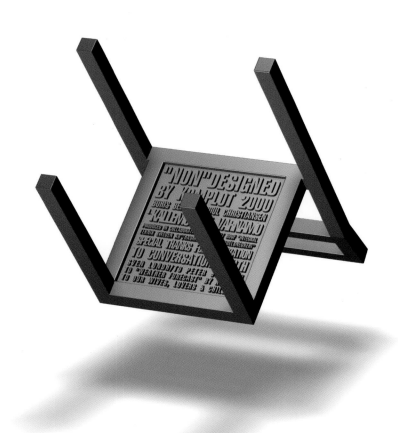

David Trubridge
Indoor/outdoor bench, Raft
American oak
h. 30cm (11⁷⁄₈in) w. 90cm (35¹⁄₂in)
l. 170cm (67in)
Limited batch production

Aptero Oy
Lamp, Secto
Laminated woodstrips
h. 60cm (23⁵⁄₈in) di. 45cm (17³⁄₄in)
Aptero Oy, Finland

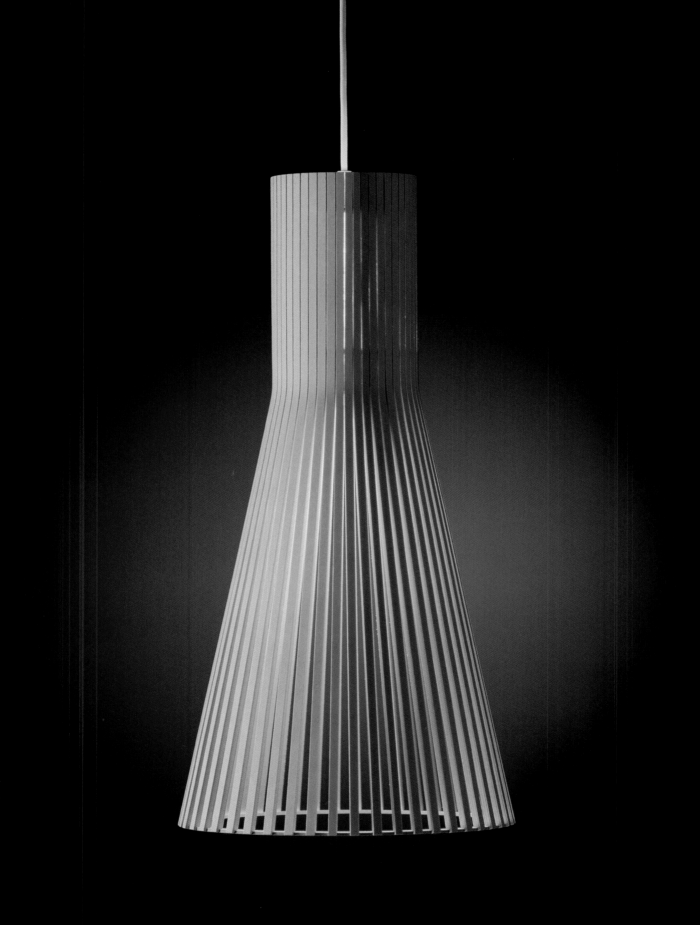

Jan Konings
Chest Box
Birch plywood
h. 60cm (23³⁄₈in) l. 60cm (23³⁄₈in)
w. 40cm (15⁵⁄₈in)
Droog Design, the Netherlands

Alfredo Häberli
Bed, Legnoletto
Wood, Aluminium
h. 37cm (14¹⁄₂in)
w. 90/140/160/180cm
(35¹⁄₂/55¹⁄₈/63/70⁷⁄₈in)
l. 212cm (83¹⁄₂in)
Alias SpA, Italy

The ubiquitous Italian designer Alfredo Häberli appeared in many leading manufacturers' collections in 2001. BD Ediciones de Diseno, Luceplan, Offect, Cappellini, Rorstand and Trunz all showcased new products by Häberli, and the designer exhibited at the Milan, Stockholm and New York furniture fairs. His wooden bed for Alias, 'Legnoletto', has the aesthetic purity and honesty characteristic of much of his best work. The modular 'Legnoletto' is construct-ed in various widths and with a choice of bed heads and bottoms, with the mattress sitting on an uncomplicated frame of struts and slats. What lifts the bed above the ordinary, however, is the graphic quality of the cut beams, which have the practical advantage of allowing air to cir-culate. Although Häberli prides himself on keeping abreast of the latest technologies, the integrity of his original idea is always para-mount: 'If the use of technology or a specific technique helps to create a more intelligent object, then I appreciate this … but often I prefer a product [that is] well executed in a traditional way. Sometimes it is better to consciously use a "prehistoric" technique in our virtual world.'

Marcel Wanders
Armchair, Fish Net Chair
Graphitic carbon rope
h. 74cm (28⅞in) w. 82cm (32in)
d. 75cm (29¼in)
Cappellini SpA, Italy

Yamaha Product Design Laboratory
Electric Upright Bass, Yamaha Silent
Bass SLB-100
Maple, spruce, mahogany, beech,
aluminium, ebony
h. 43.5cm (17in) w. 52.5cm (20½in)
l. 173.5cm (67⅝in)
Yamaha Corporation Ltd, Japan

PLASTICS

One hundred years ago cars, aeroplanes and cameras were made largely of wood. Fifty years ago they were made predominantly of metal. Today they are more likely to be made out of some kind of plastic. The reason for this is principally one of economics, owing to the hyper-efficiency of replicating large numbers of articles in plastic to satisfy the demands of an ever-expanding global society. Synthetic polymers are capable of emulating the physical properties of many materials – from glass to ceramics; they can be made rigid or flexible, aerated or dense, opaque, translucent or transparent; they can even conduct electricity and emit light.

Today it would be impossible to remove plastics from society and still retain some form of civilized existence. Plastics underpin many of the everyday services upon which we all depend, from the packaging of liquids and foodstuffs to the sealing of blood and medical supplies. The ubiquity of plastics, however, has its downside, as designers race to identify domestic products that were once made of more traditional materials and to redesign them in plastics in order to fulfil the constant demand for marketable ideas. Personally I find it very difficult to get worked up about novelty plastic objects, even those celebrated in the design press. For all their humility, such items are often almost decadent in their concept or making.

All the same, there is an enormous cultural and commercial future in plastics as they continue to permeate the realms of architecture, transportation, clothing, aerospace and so on. Ecological questions will remain only if we encourage the proliferation of cheap, useless objects – from toys to consumer durables – that senselessly exploit our precious resources. Design that values the material itself when united with intelligent humanism will always be of relevance and thereby transcends the debate. In the future there could be a system of material designation based on an article's 'life'. It could become mandatory for perishable goods to be packaged in recycled and biodegradable materials. In this way, more valuable, virgin materials could be saved for crucial applications such as the packaging of medical supplies.

Werner Aisslinger
Chair, Gel Chair
Technogel, steel, nylon
h. 75cm (29½in) w. 50cm (19⅝in)
d. 60cm (23⅝in)
Cappellini SpA, Italy

Gabriela Nahlikova and
Leona Matejkova
Vase, Elastic Vase
Epoxid
h. 40cm (15⅝in) di. 20cm (7⅞in)
Prototype

Jean-Marc Gady
Lamp, Punch-Light
Silicone
22w fluorescent bulb
h. 7cm (2¾in) di. 26cm (10¼in)
Prototype

Young Czech duo Gabriela
Nahlikova and Leona Matejkova
have reinterpreted the vase in the
rubber-like material epoxid.

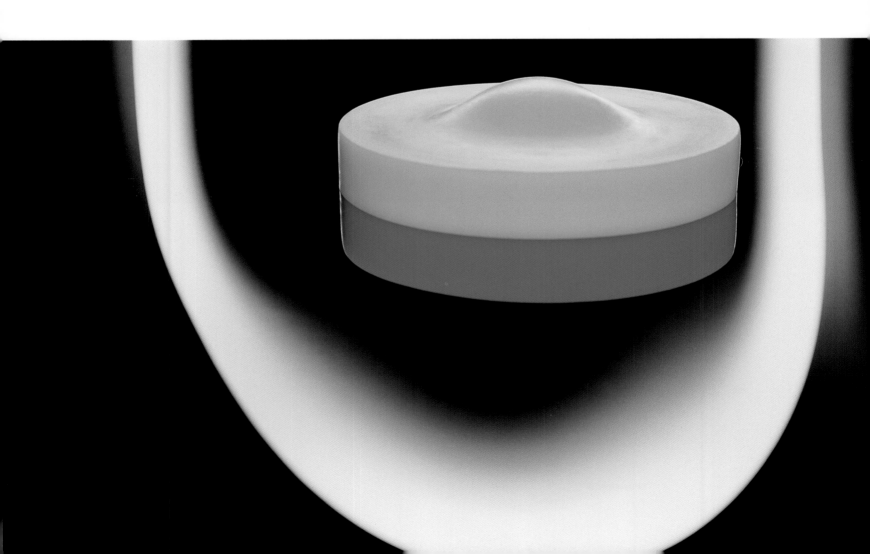

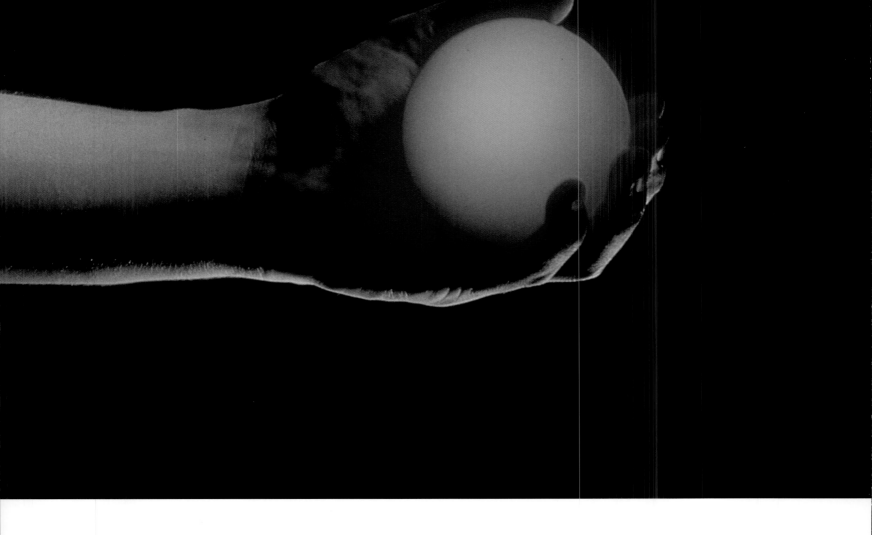

With its squeeze on/squeeze off
bubble light, Mathmos has produced the ultimate anti-stress
device. The lamp is charged
through a long white cable,
from which it can be suspended
or draped across the floor. The
'Bubble' light contains blue, green
or orange LEDs; the light is dif-
fused through silicone, creating
a richly coloured glow.

174

Aaron Rincover, Mathmos Design Team
Lamp, Bubble Light
Silicone
di. 8cm (3⅛in)
4 LEDs and rechargeable battery
Mathmos Ltd, UK

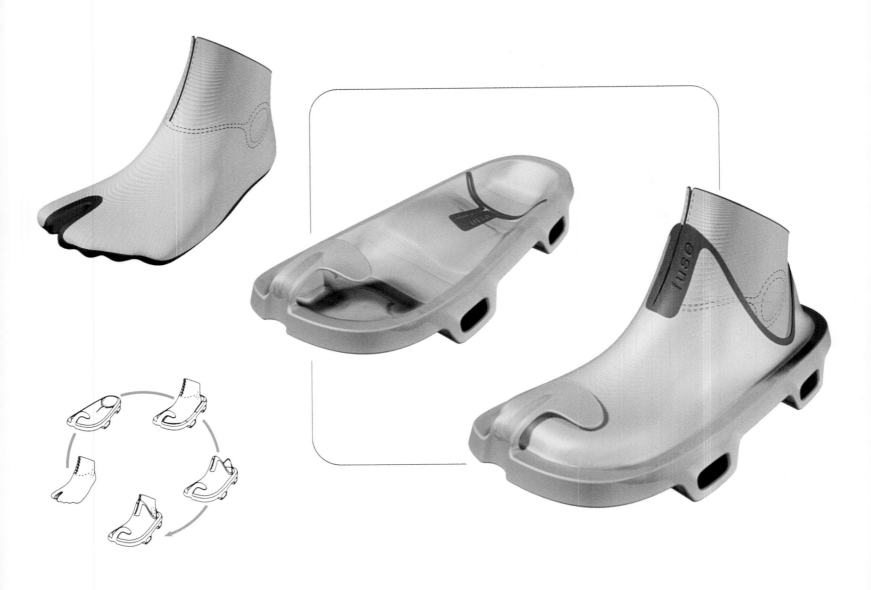

Yves Béhar/Fuseproject, Johan Liden,
Geoffrey Petrizzi
Future shoe concept, Fuse Shoe
(Tabi Clog)
Memory hybrid latex nylon exterior,
moisture wicking cotton interior layer
h. 14cm (5½in) w. 14cm (5½in)
l. 32cm (12½in)
San Francisco Museum of Modern Art,
USA
Prototype

Yves Béhar/Fuseproject, Johan Liden,
Phil Grebe
Future shoe concept, Learning Shoe
Memory hybrid latex nylon exterior,
moisture wicking cotton interior layer
h. 14cm (5½in) w. 14cm (5½in)
l. 32cm (12½in)
San Francisco Museum of Modern Art,
USA
Prototype

Yves Béhar was approached by the
San Francisco Museum of Modern
Art to come up with two pairs
of sneakers for the year 2005.
'Learning Shoe' and 'Fuse Shoe'
formed part of an exhibition curat-
ed by Aaron Betsky and Steven
Skov Holt which showcased the
innovative shoe design and technology of the last five years as well
as illustrating possible conceptual
developments for the future. The
'Learning Shoe' actually processes

information about the wearer,
hardening or softening to suit
individual pressure points in order
to prevent wear and bad posture.
The soft material and a microchip
imbedded in the sole react to the
individual's habits. The chip also
sends these details back to the
manufacturer, allowing the creation of completely customized
shoes. Today's sneakers are made
from a variety of materials, which
makes them hard to recycle. By

contrast, Béhar's shoe for the new
millennium is crafted from one
recyclable material. The 'Fuse Shoe'
is a blend of East and West – of
the Japanese tabi slipper sock
and the ubiquitous sneaker. It is
designed to be worn both indoors
and out; a protective outer layer
reacts to both external conditions
and body temperature, while an
inner cotton sock is intended for
lounging at home.

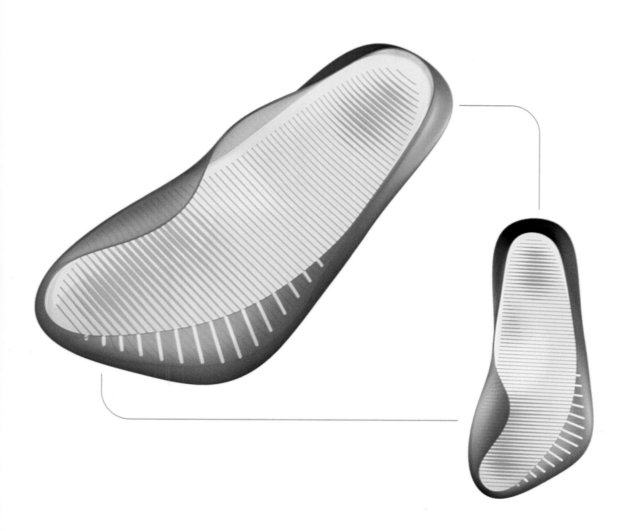
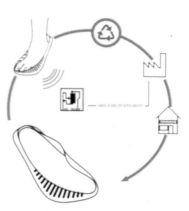

OVERLEAF
Dirk Bikkembergs
Mat
Bonded foam and vinyl
h. 4cm (1½in) w. 200cm (78in)
l. 100cm (39in)
Bulo, Belgium
Limited batch production

For this piece the Belgian office furniture manufacturer Bulo asked fashion designer Dirk Bikkembergs to redefine the boundaries between work and play. As new communication technologies advance, it is no longer necessary to conduct business from a static workplace; we can now carry on our affairs at any time and from any place. Bikkembergs's answer is the 'MAT' – a 2 x 1 metre foam pad that can be used in a flexible and mobile manner and in every conceivable situation. Its range of applications is not merely limited to just lying down; it can also be used as a soft floor covering, as a piece of seating furniture, a standing table, as a wall to lean against, or simply as a gym mat. For vertical suspension, a mounting set and a black elastic band can be ordered, the latter functioning as a magazine or newspaper holder.

177

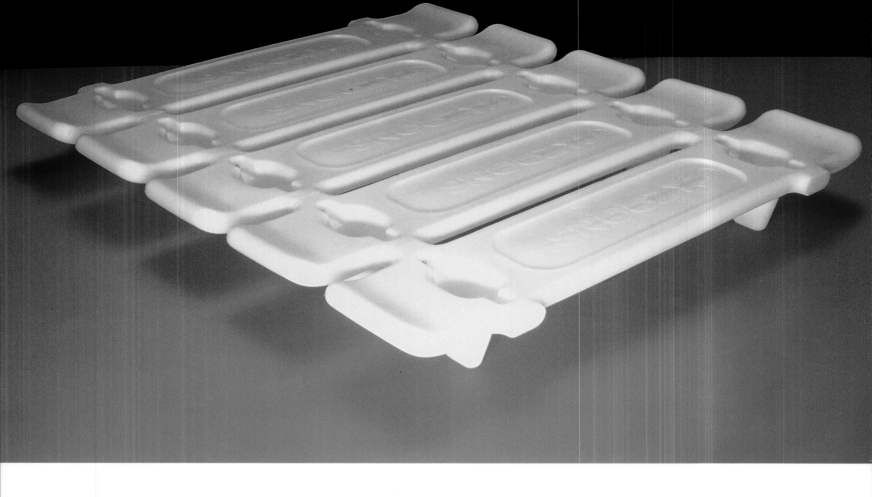

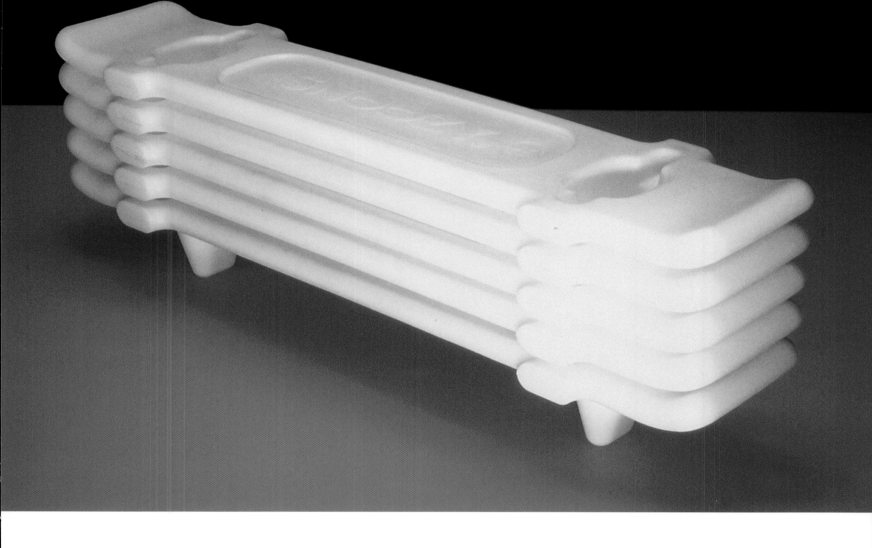

Nick Crosbie, Paul Crofts
Furniture, Snoozy
Polyethylene
h. 26.5cm (10⅛in) w. 170cm (66⅜in)
l. 260cm (101⅜in)
Inflate, UK

Jasper Morrison
Chair, Air
Polypropylene, glass fibre
h. 77.5cm (30¼in) w. 49cm (19⅛in)
d. 50cm (19½in)
Magis SpA, Italy
Prototype

Eugenio Perazza's company, Magis, was founded in the 1970s – a time when the market was flooded with 'tasteful' Italian design and when consumers were hungering for something different. Instead of ageless classic collections, there was a shift towards fashion – products that would represent a season and define individual styles. Magis is a Latin adverb meaning 'more' or 'additionally', and when placed in front of an adjective it intensifies its quality. A chair that is 'magis necessarius' is indispensable, and a bookcase that is 'magis elegans' is simply sublime. Magis also forms the basis of the word 'magisterial' – there to teach others. The products that Magis present are not based on market needs but rather on what, over the years, they have learned to do best and what they have become known for.

The company works mainly in plastics and metals and has spent a lot of money on researching new methods of working with these materials. Perazza believes that while technology may be widely accessible – anybody with enough money can afford it – it is technique that allows the designer to turn technology into a good concept and ultimately an innovative design. The company develops ideas, then commissions different designers to interpret them aesthetically. 'We want to use different vocabularies, languages and dialects', explains Perazza. He believes that if an individual is chosen who can really relate to the subject he or she has been given, then you end up with a perfect product.

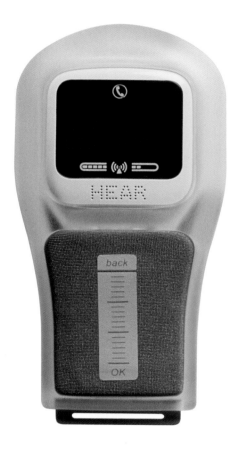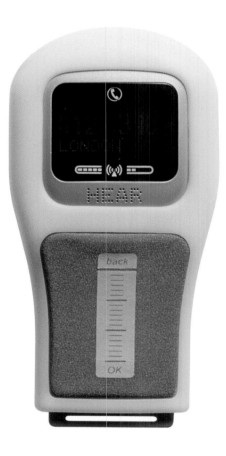

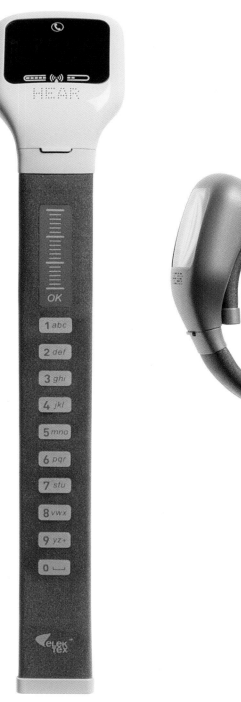
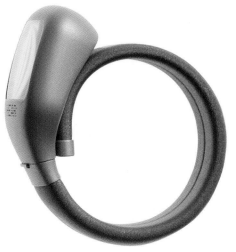

Sam Hecht, IDEO
Communication Tools, Fabrications
Elektex cloth, polyurethane,
methacrylate
Soft Wrist Phone: w. 4.6cm (1¾in)
l. 21.5cm (8⅜in) d. 1.8cm (¾in)
Electrotextiles, UK

Flick through any design magazine over the past year and you are likely to see the face of Karim Rashid staring back at you. He is the first major design figure to come out of America since Venturi and Graves, and he is certainly king of the new American wave. And with more than 800 designs in production, there is no question that Rashid is prolific.

But there is much more to Karim than simply being a well-known workaholic. He is already the author of a number of design classics – from the humble 'Garbo Can' to the 'Oh Chair', both designed for Umbra; he has been the recipient of numerous major design prizes including the George Nelson Award for breakthrough furniture design; and examples of his work can be found in most major collections worldwide. His self-proclaimed mission is to change the world and to make design democratic. He describes himself as 'trying to roll from mall to mall giving consumers interesting and affordable designs and spreading the gospel of design to middle America'. What makes his work remarkable is how his individual sense of style combines with an equally strong philosophy.

His objects, including everything from packaging to furniture, have soft and friendly organic shapes that communicate tactility and have a strong visual sense of comfort and pleasure. They are a hybrid of the emotional and the industrialization of cutting-edge technology. He is also a strong advocate of digital production – manufacturing without tooling – and many of his designs are in fact produced this way.

Zaha Hadid
Sofa, Glacier
Fire varnished wood
l. 500cm (197in) w. 125cm (49¼in)
h. 50cm (19¾in)
Sawaya & Moroni, Italy

Karim Rashid
Installation, Pleasurescape Environment
Fibreglass, automotive lacquer
l. 1219cm (480in) w. 975.3cm (384in)
One-off

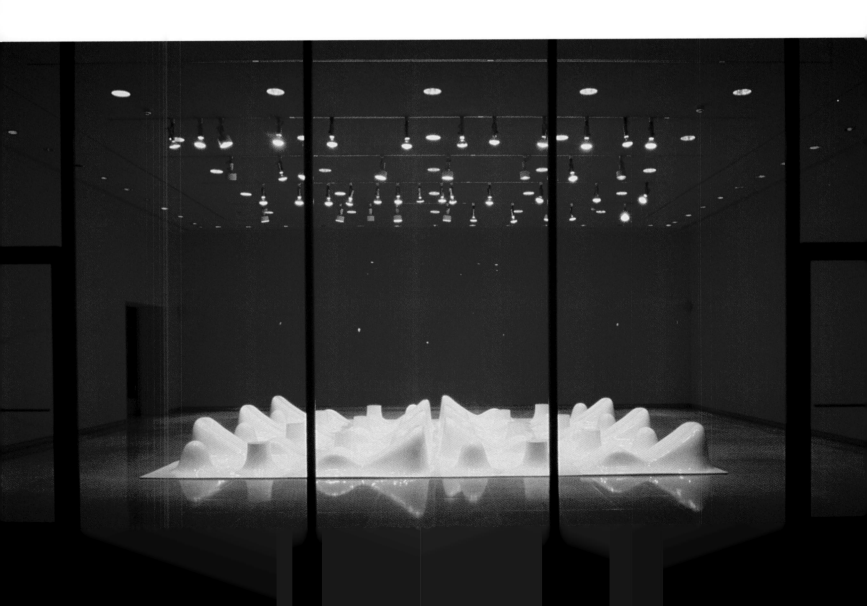

Stefano Giovannoni
Breadbin, Gnam
Thermoplastic resin
h. 16.5cm (6½in) w. 30cm (11⁷⁄₈in)
l. 46cm (18⅛in)
Alessi SpA, Italy

Scott Henderson
Salad Servers, Wovo
Injection moulded SAN
h. 4.5cm (1³⁄₄in) w. 6.3cm (2½in)
l. 33.5cm (13⅛in)
Smart Design, USA

OVERLEAF
Hannes Wettstein
Chair, Alfa
SCM (Polyester resin compound
reinforced with glass fibre)
h. 80cm (31¼in) l. 49cm (19⅛in)
w. 50cm (19½in)
Molteni & Co. SpA, Italy

Delo Lindo
Waste basket, Contenants
PVC
h. 20cm (7⁷/₈in) di. 44cm (17¹/₈in)
Limited batch production

Matt Sindall
Table, Iseeme
Steel frame, dual sheet of
polycarbonate, metallic film
h. 45cm (17³/₄in) w. 48cm (18⁷/₈in)
d. 85cm (33¹/₂in)
Prototype

Matt Sindall
Chair, Chromatique
Wooden frame, lenticular film
h. 160cm (63in) w. 96cm (37⁷/₈in)
d. 93cm (36⁵/₈in)
Prototype

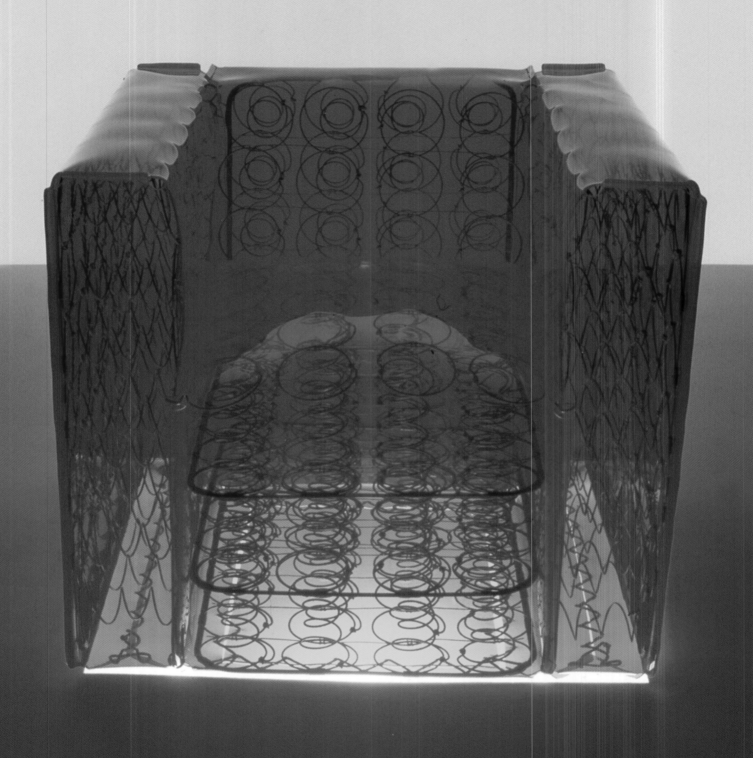

Ennemlaghi Ltd
Armchair, Red Cube
Steel, transparent PVC
h. 90.8cm (35³⁄₈in) w. 90.8cm
(35³⁄₈in) d. 90.8cm (35³⁄₈in)
Ennemlaghi Ltd, UK

NL Architects
Straps, designed for Mandarina Duck
Rhodorsil Melange-Maitre MF 345 U
w. 3cm (1¹⁄₈in) l. 70cm (27⁵⁄₈in)
d. 1cm (³⁄₈in)
Droog Design, the Netherlands

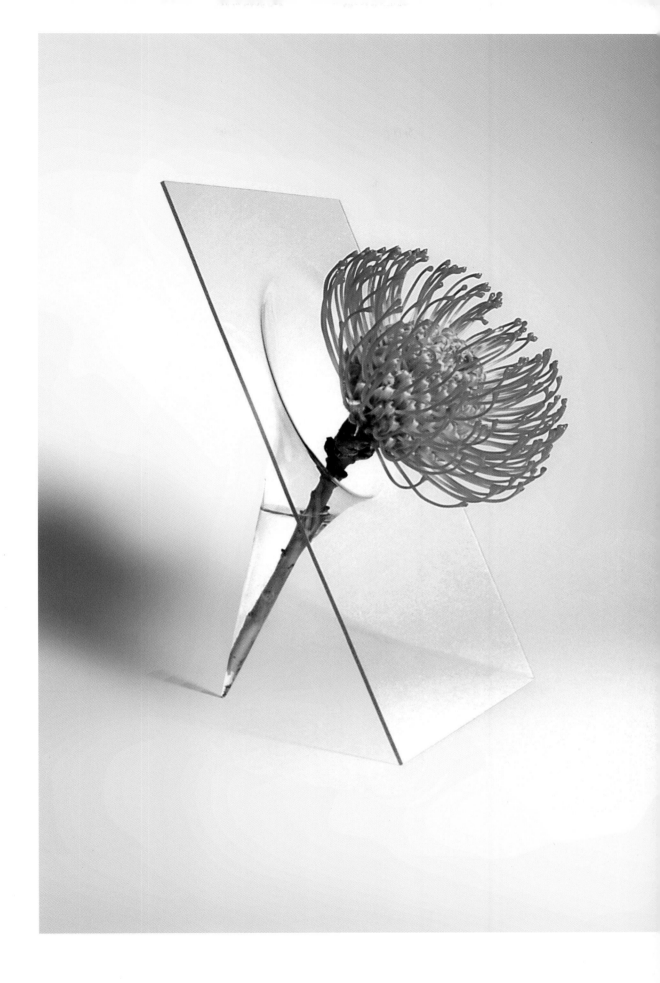

Tokujin Yoshioka
Lighting system
Fibre optic technology
NTT-X, Japan

Joris Sparenberg
Vanishing vase
PET recyclable plastic
h. 20.5cm (8^{1}/$_{8}$in) w. 14cm (5^{1}/$_{2}$in)
d. 10cm (4in)
Counterpoint, USA

Karim Rashid
Chair, Sloop
Thermo formed acrylic
Idée, Japan

Luca Bonato
Vase, Numero 1
Acrylic
h. 13cm (5$\frac{1}{8}$in) w. 13cm (5$\frac{1}{8}$in)
d. 13cm (5$\frac{1}{8}$in)
Fusina snc, Italy

Toshiyuki Kita
LCD TV, LC-20C1/LC-15C1/LC-13C1
Plastic
h. 48.3/37.4/40cm (19/14³/₄/15³/₄in)
w. 47.7/36.9/33.4cm (18³/₄/14¹/₂/13¹/₈in)
d. 6.5/5.8/5.7cm (2¹/₂/2¹/₄/2¹/₄in)
Sharp Corporation, Japan

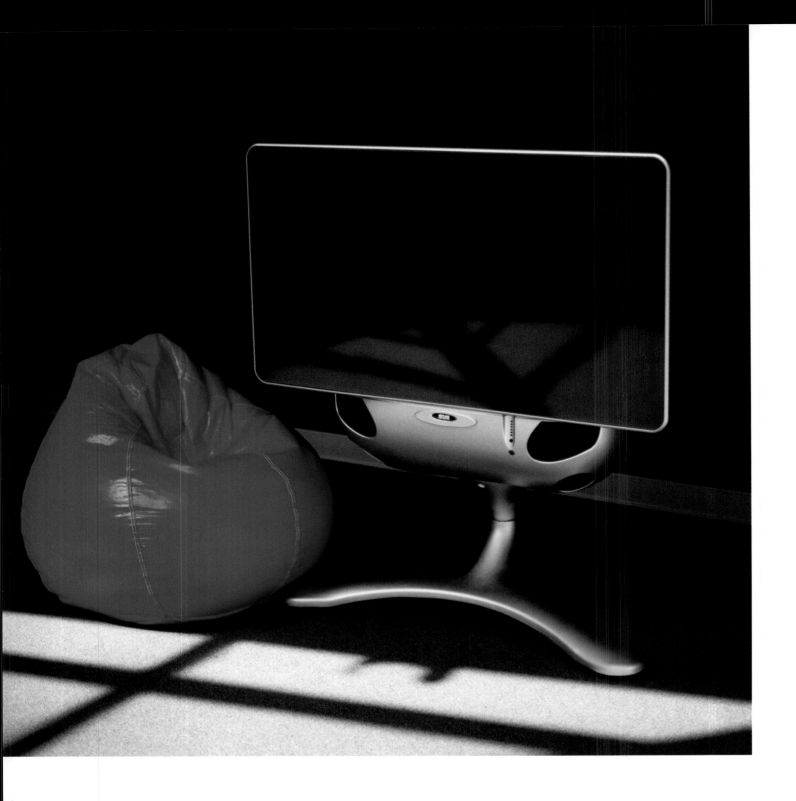

Stephen Peart
Rear projected high definition television,
HDTV 50" diagonal
ABS, thermoplastic, aluminium
h. 120cm (40in) w. 120cm (40in)
d. 44cm (17in)
Digital Reflection Inc., USA

Hidetoshi Fujimoto
Cellular Phone, J-SHO4
ABS
h. 12.7cm (5in) w. 3.9cm (1 1/2in)
d. 1.7cm (5/8in)
Sharp Corporation, Japan

Theo Williams
Calculator, Handy Calculator
Silicone rubber, aluminium
h. 12.8cm (5in) w. 7.2cm (2 ⁷/₈in)
d. 1.1cm (³/₈in)
Lexon, France

Theo Williams
Travel lock, Handy Lock
Steel, rubber casing
h. 6.2cm (2¹/₂in) w. 4cm (1⁵/₈in)
d. 1.2cm (¹/₂in)
Lexon, France

Tim Thom
Keyboard of Interactive TV, TAK
ABS
h. 7cm (2³/₄in) w. 31.5cm (12³/₈in)
l 12.5cm (5in)
Thomson Multimedia, France

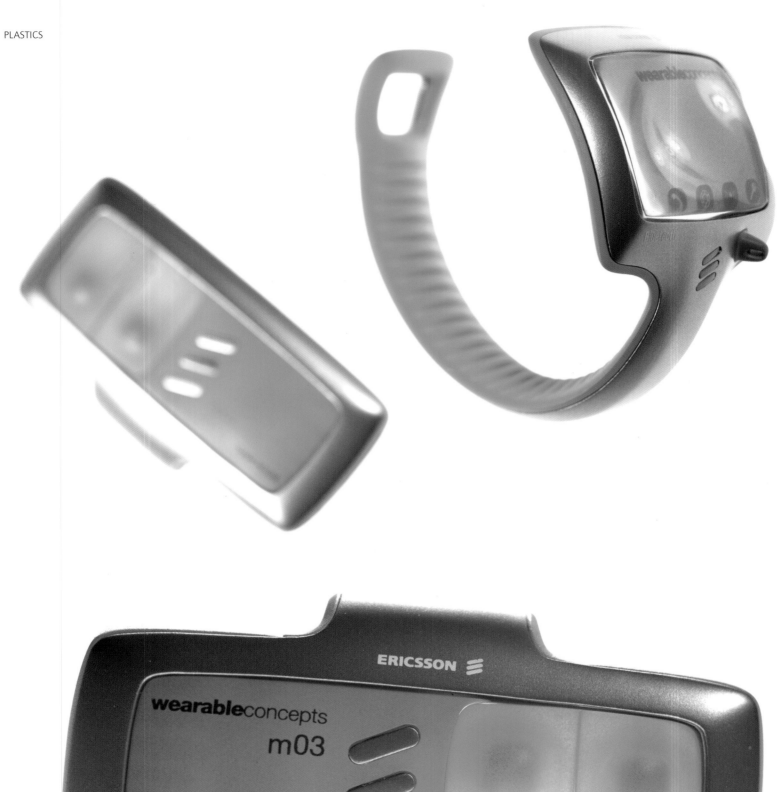

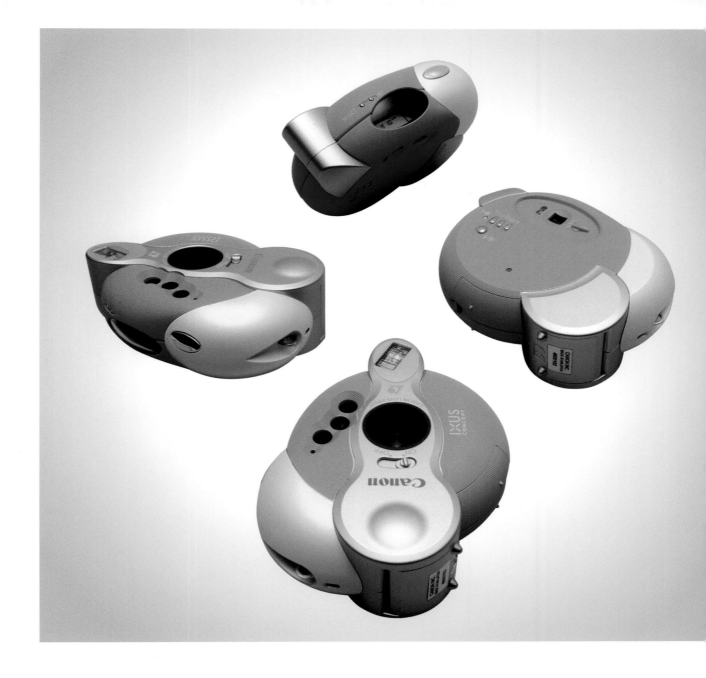

Thomas Meyerhoffer
Interactive Wrist Display, m03 Ericsson
Moulded aluminium, soft-touch
elastomer, crystal, plastic
One size spring aluminium clasp
Display: h. 4cm (1¹/₂in) w. 5.3cm (2in)
d. 0.7cm (¹/₄in)
Ericsson, Sweden

Yasushi Shiotani
APS compact camera, IXUS concept
Arancia
PC/ABS, PC
h. 8.6cm (3³/₈in) w. 10.9cm (4¹/₄in)
d. 3.9cm (1¹/₂in)
Canon Inc. Design Centre, Japan

Herbst LaZar Bell
Innovative wearable technology, Aura
Polypropylene
Digital Beads: h. 2.5cm (1in)
w. 2.5cm (1in) d. 2.5cm (1in)
ID Clip: h. 5cm (2in) w. 5cm (2in)
d. 2.5cm (1in)
Cameo: h. 12cm (5in) w. 2.5cm (1in)
d. 2.5cm (1in)
Herbst LaZar Bell Inc., USA
Prototype

An increasing range of wearable technology has become available over the past couple of years, but Aura's range of fashionable smart items goes one step further. It is no longer necessary to wear chunky items of clothing with cell phone, pager and so on sewn into the sleeve; Aura have designed items that morph fashion and technology into one, creating unique pieces that adapt individually to the wearer and, on first glance, give no hint of their function. 'Digital Beads' tie hair up into playful shapes, but they also contain a microchip that can be activated to download biodata about the wearer. 'ID Clip' is a barrette that, once engaged by inserting the pin through the clip, acts as a digital identification and banking communications system. Sensors on the pin recognize the wearer through a stored fingerprint, and transactions can be made by scanning a personal barcode. 'Cameo' is an item of jewellery that stores 3-D body data and shopping information. It scans clothing tags, applying the information to the 3-D data and producing a holographic image of the wearer in the selected outfit. 'Living Shirt' is made from heat-sensitive fabric, and the sleeves automatically open and close to adapt to environmental conditions. The Aura philosophy is that technology should be fun and invisible so as to be unintimidating and unintrusive.

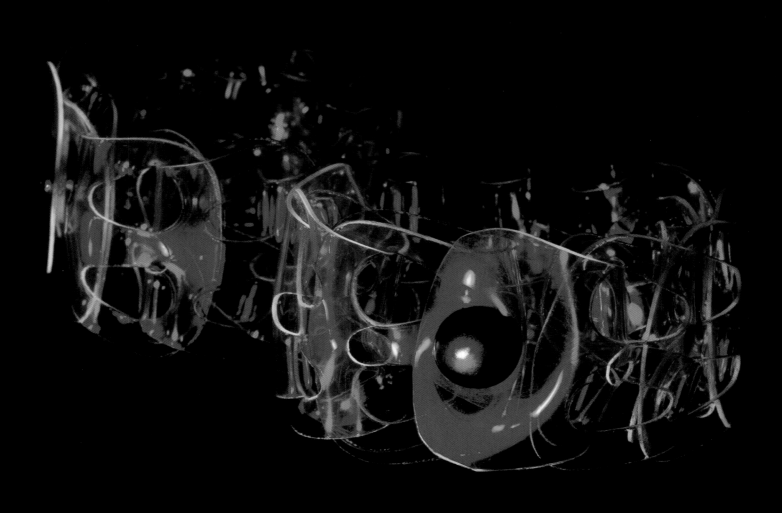

Sonia Rykiel
Bracelet, Medusa
Plastic, fluorescent pigment
Sonia Rykiel, France

Jean-Charles de Castelbajac
Hairgrips, Octopus
Plastic, fluorescent pigment
J.C de Castelbajac, France

ABOVE
Masayo Ave
Wall carpet, Sahara
Industrial wool felt, DuPont Corian®
w. 60cm (23⁵/₈in) l. 180cm (71in)
Masayo Ave Creation, Switzerland
One-off

FACING
Masayo Ave
Wall carpet, La Mia Africa
Industrial wool felt, DuPont Corian®
w. 45cm (17³/₄in) l. 210cm (82³/₄in)
Masayo Ave Creation, Switzerland
One-off

Masayo Ave's 'Sahara' and 'La Mia Africa' illustrate the talent she has developed over the last few years for juxtaposing contrasting yet complimentary materials – in this instance, industrial felt and Corian (see page 219) – to produce highly individual and sensual pieces. The results of these unusual combinations are often unexpected and have a direct emotional appeal. The 'industrial ivory' of the Corian and the dark, rough appearance of felt reminded Ave of an elephant, inspiring her to create these 'African' wall hangings.

PREVIOUS PAGE
Ronan and Erwan Bouroullec
Console with Mirror
Corian®
h. 80cm (31¹/₄in) w. 200cm (78in)
d. 45cm (17¹/₄in)
Cappellini SpA, Italy

Ronan and Erwan Bouroullec
Console with bowl
Corian®
h. 55cm (21¹/₂in) w. 200cm (78in)
d. 45cm (17¹/₂in)
Cappellini SpA, Italyl

LEFT
Ross Lovegrove
Organic Form Series One
Corian®
DuPont, USA

Corian was without a doubt *the* material of the 2001 Milan Furniture Fair. Although this advanced blend of mineral and pure acrylic polymer was launched in 1966, it is only now coming into its own, as architects and designers increasingly turn to it to create furniture, lighting and interiors for a wide range of sectors. The manufacturers of Corian, DuPont, approached many leading designers to create objects for the Milan fair, including Masayo Ave, who contributed delicate textile wall hangings, and Ettore Sottsass, whose monumental show of abstract architectural elements was entitled 'Exercises in Another Material'. Cappellini also displayed work using Corian by a group of renowned international designers – Marc Newson, Ronan and Erwan Bouroullec and Jasper Morrison – setting out to show how the material's design potential can inspire innovative functional furniture and accessories for both home and commercial environments. White was chosen for all of the pieces in order to emphasize the workable qualities and versatility of this translucent, cool-to-the-touch material.

The new, complex design shapes now being produced by CAD programs are demanding increasingly more malleable materials. Corian appears to be the perfect answer to such demands: it can be worked into virtually any shape or design, whether a softly rounded ergonomic table or a long reception desk. The Bouroullec brothers have been especially innovative in their use of what they term a 'monochromatic monomaterial', sculpting vases, platters and mirrors out of the body of their 'Tavolo' and 'Tavolino' designs.

Biographies

Werner Aisslinger was born in Berlin in 1964. He founded his own design company in 1993 and since then has carried out various furniture projects for Italian companies such as Cappellini, Magis and Porro. His 'endless shelf' won the Bundespreis Product Design and in 1997 his 'Juli' chair for Cappellini was acquired as part of the permanent collection at MoMA, New York. Aisslinger has also worked on corporate architecture concepts and projects for Lufthansa and Mercedes Benz. 172–3

Flavia Alves de Souza was born in Brazil in 1969 and graduated from the University of Belo Horizonte in 1992. She then worked as a jewellery designer. In 1994 she undertook an MA at the Milan Polytechnic and subsequently worked with Iosa Ghini, Anna Gili, Marco Zanini and Sottsass Associati. Her design work includes silver for Pamploni, glassware for Egizia, interiors for Muraoka, Japan and porcelain for Rosenthal. 115

Masayo Ave was born in Tokyo in 1962 but has lived in Milan for the past decade. She graduated in architecture from Hosei University in Japan and after practising for a few years moved to Milan where in 1990 she completed an MA in Industrial Design at the Domus Academy. In 1992 she established Ave Design Corporation, based in Tokyo and Milan, and has since won various awards, including the ICFF 2000 editor's award. Clients have included international companies such as Authentics while her own design collection was launched by Atrox GmbH in 2000. In 2001 she started to collaborate with DuPont. 214, 215

Jacob de Baan graduated from the Gerrit Rietveld Academy in 1987 and worked in Amsterdam until 1991 when he moved to Germany to work for Team Buchin Design. He moved back to Amsterdam in 1995 and set up the D4 Agency whose clients include the Dutch Ministry of Finance, Jumbo, NOVEM, Osram and Philips. 80, 81

Gijs Bakker was born in 1942. He graduated from the Gerrit Rietveld Academy and then worked at Royal Van Kempen & Begeer. Bakker co-founded the innovative Droog Design group which works with major international companies. 33

Barber Osgerby is a design consultancy that was founded in 1996 by Edward Barber and Jay Osgerby. Barber Osgerby have created products for companies such as Cappellini, Isokon Plus, Offecct and Asplund. Named best designers at I.C.F.F in New York in 1998, Barber and Osgerby are also Creative Directors of Universal – the practice they founded in 2001 to oversee their interior design and architecture projects. Barber Osgerby have also developed a significant body of conceptual and advisory work. Recent projects include an innovative bathroom environment for Dornbracht, a display concept for Levi's and a graphic design for Abet Laminati. 140

Yves Béhar was born in Switzerland in 1967 and studied at the Art Centre College of Design in Southern California. He is design principal and founder of Fuseproject and works in many fields, including personal care, technology, fashion, home goods and experimental projects. Clients include Alcatel, Birkenstock, Hewlett Packard, Nissan, Nike, Microsoft and and he has won many awards. His work can be seen at the San Francisco Museum of Modern Art. 58–9, 176, 177

Tamar Ben David is an Israeli designer. She is now based in Italy where she has collaborated with such companies as Serafino Zani, Zanotta and Ycami. 16

Markus Benesch was born in Munich in 1969. He studied in Birmingham, England and later at the Domus Academy in Milan, since which time he has been active in the fields of interior and product design. He set up the 'Money for Milan' initiative in 1995 and since then has exhibited regularly. 150, 151

Dirk Bikkembergs was born in Germany in 1959. He studied fashion at the Antwerp Academy for the Arts and went on to become one of the internationally renowned 'Antwerp Six' group of fashion designers. Since then he has diversified into other areas of design. 178–9

Luca Bonata was born in Marostica, Italy in 1962. Since 1984 he has worked in the family workshop with Plexiglas, making jewellery. He has exhibited often and since 1992 has worked solely with Plexiglas, making sculptures and objects. His work has been used in films and won him a gold medal in Munich at the Handwerkmesse in 1994. He is based in Bassano del Grappa, Italy. 201

Erwan Bouroullec was born in Quimper, France in 1976 and studied industrial design at the Ecole Nationale Superieure des Arts Appliques and the Ecole Nationale des Arts Decoratifs. He has been collaborating with his brother, Ronan, since 1998.

Ronan Bouroullec was born in 1971 in Quimper, France. He graduated in applied and decorative art and has worked on a freelance basis since 1995, designing objects and furniture for Cappellini, Liaigre, Domeau et Peres, Ex Novo, Ligne Roset and Galerie Neotu. In 1999 he was awarded Best Designer at the ICFF in New York. 92–3, 216–17

Laurene Leon Boym was born and brought up in New York where she studied at the School of Visual Arts and the Pratt Institute, graduating in 1993. Since 1994 she has been a partner in Boym Partners Inc., whose clients have included Authentics, Swatch, Vitra and the Cooper-Hewitt National Design Museum in New York. Her work encompasses product, interior design and installations, examples of which are held in the permanent collection of MoMA, New York. Laurene Leon Boym was a founder of the Association of Women Industrial Designers and has taught product design at the Parsons School of Design since 1994. 110

Debbie Jane Buchan was born in Edinburgh in 1973. She studied textiles in Aberdeen, followed by an MA in Surface Communication, from which she graduated in 1996. She now works for AVA CAD/CAM, who produce bespoke software for the textile and decorative industries. In her own work she is concerned with 'smart' fabrics and pushing the boundaries between design disciplines through the innovative use of new and existing applications and technologies. 114, 118

Humberto Campana trained as a lawyer but in 1983 teamed up with his architect brother Fernando, to form one of the most interesting design duos active today. Based in São Paolo, Brazil, the siblings were thrust into the limelight with their 1989 exhibition 'The Inconsolable'. The brothers' work produces emphatically political rather than merely functional objects and explores the possibility of social redemption in an impoverished society. Hence their radical vision involves the use of humble, traditional materials and industrial surplus in an attempt to create an independent Brazilian language of design. They participated in the 1995 exhibition in Milan, 'Brazil makes Design Hip'. Their work has been exhibited widely, and their clients include Edra and O Luce. 48–9, 116–17, 156, 157

Fabio Carlesso has worked as a graphic and interior designer since 1987. His main inspiration is contemporary art and he is particularly interested in the use and application of resins and plastics. He works on a consulting basis with various Italian architects and textile companies. 162

Casimir was born in Koersel (Belgium) in 1966 and studied industrial design in Genk, graduating in 1991. Since 1995 he has worked in furniture design and in 1997 he expanded into architecture, interior design, product development and graphic design. 38

Jean-Charles de Castelbajac is a Parisian couturier. Born in 1949, he has been creating garments since the age of 19, searching for a pure, elemental visual language. In 1979 he began diversifying into other areas of design and has recently worked with Ligne Roset. He has taught at Central Saint Martins School of Art & Design, London and the Academy of Applied Arts, Vienna. 213

Antonio Citterio was born in Meda, Italy in 1950 and has been involved in design since 1967. He studied at Milan Polytechnic and set up a studio with Paolo Nava in 1973. Amongst others, they have worked for B&B Italia and Flexform, while in 1979 they were awarded the Compasso d'Oro. In 1987 Terry Dwan became a partner and projects have included schemes for Esprit, as well as offices and showrooms for Vitra. In partnership with Toshiyuka Kita, their work in Japan has included the Kobe headquarters of World Company, the Corente Building and the Diago Headquarters in Tokyo. He has taught at the Domus Academy in Milan. Recent projects include interior architecture for Cerruti, Emanuel Ungaro SA, the UEFA headquarters, B&B Italia and a Zegna sports store. In 1999 Antonio Citterio & Partners was established as a multi-disciplinary architecture and design studio with offices in Milan and Hamburg. 21

Kenneth Cobonpue was born in the Philippines and trained as an industrial designer in New York. He then returned to the Philippines, where he runs Interior Crafts of the Islands Inc. in Cebu City with his mother, Betty. The company started as a hobby, but they have since won three Philippine industry awards for their contemporary, sculptural use of rattan in the field of furniture design. 154, 155

Claudio Colucci was born in Switzerland in 1965 and now lives and works between Paris and Tokyo. His design clients have included Martin Margiela, Issey Miyake, Habitat, Idée (Japan) and Thomson Multimedia. 131

Nick Crosbie is one of the founder partners of the London design company Inflate. Born in 1971, he studied at Central Saint Martins College of Art & Design and the Royal College of Art, London. Inflate was established in 1995 and has since gained international acclaim. Paul Crofts was born in 1973 and joined Inflate in 1997, where he is now Senior Designer. 180, 181

Helle Damkjær is an industrial and graphic designer. After several years of collaboration with companies in Milan, London, Düsseldorf and Chicago, she is now based in Paris. Her style is characterized by a skilful combination of graphic and industrial design, clean aesthetics and optimum functionality. 30

Delo Lindo was founded by Fabien Cagani and Laurent Matras. Both were born in 1961 and studied at the Ecole Nationale Superieure des Arts Decoratifs de Paris. Operating within the fields of design and interior architecture they formed Delo Lindo in 1985, since which time their clients have included Soca Line, Ligne Roset and Cinna. In 1993 they won the Grand Prix of the Press Internationale de la Critique du Meuble. Based in Paris, they have exhibited widely throughout Europe. 50, 51, 194

Michele De Lucchi was born in Ferrara in 1951. He belongs to a particular generation of architects who have won great international renown and was a leading force in the Cavart Group during the Radical Design years. De Lucchi was a founder member of the Memphis group which made a huge contribution towards the new design movement of the eighties. Today his Milan studio conducts a number of activities from the design of industrial objects to furnishings, designing interiors and architectural works for both public and private use. Clients include Arflex, Artemide, Kartell, Pelikan, Deutsche Bank, Olivetti and many others. 34, 82, 83, 84, 85, 128, 144, 145

Eric DeWitt studied furniture design at the Rhode Island School of Design and graduated in 2001. He has exhibited his work in New York and Milan and is curently working for Swing, a design firm in Concord, Massachusetts. 126

Charles and Ray Eames are among the most important American designers of the twentieth century, renowned for their contribution to architecture, furniture design, industrial design and photography. Charles Eames was born in 1907 and started his own architectural office in 1930. As his design ideas spread beyond architecture, he received a fellowship to Cranbrook Academy of Art where he became head of design. Ray Kaiser Eames was born around 1913 and studied painting in New York before moving to Cranbook. She and Charles married in 1941. After the war their work began to be produced by Herman Miller and Vitra. Most famous are the Lounge Chair and Ottoman from 1956, while their Tandem Sling Seating is still in use in airports across the world. Charles died in 1978 and Ray in 1988. Their office still operates and they are a major influence on many design disciplines. 132

Norman Foster was born in Manchester in 1935 and studied at Manchester University and Yale University. In 1967 he founded Foster Associates. He is renowned for his hi-tech designs, such as the Hong Kong and Shanghai Banks (1979–85) and Stansted Airport (1981–9). More recent projects have included the Sackler Galleries at the Royal Academy of Arts, London, the Centre d'Art Cultural, Nimes, the remodelling of the Reichstag in Berlin, Chek Lap Kok Airport in Hong Kong, Canary Wharf Station and the Millennium Bridge in London. Although primarily concerned with large scale projects, Foster is also active in furniture and product design. 32

Jean-Marc Gady lives and works in Paris. After studying interior architecture and environmental design at the Ecole Bleue in Paris, he worked as a freelance designer of websites, packaging and products. His clients have included Nestlé, France Telecom, Sephora and Ligne Roset. He has won several prizes and also teaches at the Ecole Bleue. 172

Jakob Gebert was born in Freiburg, Germany in 1965. In 1994 he graduated in interior, product and building design from the HFG Basle and since then has run his own atelier for industrial design and exhibition architecture. Clients have included Belux, Nile Holger Moorman and Vitra. He has won many prizes and has taught in Basle and Karlsruhe. 141

Christian Ghion was born in Montmorency, France in 1958. He graduated from Etude de Creation de Mobilier, Paris in 1987 and since then has worked with Patrick Nadeau. In 1998 he initiated his own project, concentrating on industrial and interior design for European and Japanese companies such as Cinna/Roset, Neotu, 3 Suisses, Idée, Tendo and Thierry Mugler. He has won several awards and his work is on show in major museums in New York, Los Angeles and Paris. 128

Stefano Giovannoni was born in La Spezia, Italy in 1954 and graduated in architecture from the University of Florence in 1978. From 1978 to 1990 he lectured and researched at the University of Florence and also taught at the Domus Academy, Milan and the Institute of Design in Reggio Milano. He is the founding member of King-Kong Production, which is concerned with avant-garde research in design, interiors, fashion and architecture. Clients include Alessi, Cappellini and Tisca, France. 190

Eric Gizard was born in Cambodia in 1960 and now lives in Paris where he runs Eric Gizard Associés. His clients include SNCF, Groupe Air France, Ministère de Affaires Etrangeres, Daum, D'Argentat and Asiatides. 102

Johanna Grawunder was born in San Diego in 1961 and studied architecture at the California Polytechnic, in San Luis Obispo and Florence. She has worked with Sottsass Associati since 1985, becoming a partner in 1989, but she also works independently in interior and lighting design. Since 1994 she has been working in glass and cut crystal with Salviati. Recent architectural work has included the Habustan Bar, Jerusalem (1998) and the Milan offices of BRW & Partners (1998–9). She has lectured at the Domus Academy, Milan and the Royal College of Art, London. 67, 68–9, 73

Alfredo Häberli was born in Buenos Aires, Argentina in 1964 but moved to Switzerland in 1977. He studied industrial design in Zurich and worked as an installation designer at the Museum für Gestaltung until 1993. Since then he has worked for companies such as Cappellini, Asplund, Alias, Edra, Zanotta, Thonet, Driade, Zeritalia and Bally. He works alone or in collaboration with Christophe Marchand. 167

Zaha Hadid is a London-based architectural designer whose work comprises urban and product design as well as interior and furniture design. Her drawings, designs and structures have won worldwide recognition and numerous awards including several first prizes for her design of the Cardiff Bay Opera House, Wales (1994). Hadid was born in Baghdad in 1950 and studied at the American University in Beirut and the Architectural Association in London. She then worked with the Office for Metropolitan Architecture and set up her own practice in 1979. In 1982 Hadid won the Architectural Gold Design Medal and in 1983 the Hong Kong Peak International Design Competition. Notable projects include the Vitra Fire Station, Weil am Rhein, Germany (1991–3), the Contemporary Arts Centre in Cincinnati and an Exhibition Pavilion, also in Weil am Rhein (1999). 188

Isabel Hamm studied ceramics in Germany before moving to London where she graduated with an MA in ceramics and glass from the Royal College of Art in 1998. Since then she has worked freelance in Cologne and her clients include Salviati, Iceberg

Home Collection and Schott Glass. In 1998 she won the RSA Student Design Award. 79

Harry & Camila Vega met while studying for an MA at the Domus Academy in Milan. Harry was born in the Netherlands in 1966 and Camila in Chile in 1971. Harry studied at the Design Academy in Eindhoven while Camila graduated in fashion design from the Marangoni Institute. In 1998 they established Studio Harry & Camila and have produced textiles, lighting and furniture. Their client list includes Alessi, Idée, Fontana Arte and Leonardo Glass. 90, 104, 120

Sam Hecht is an interior and industrial designer. Born in London in 1969, he studied at the Royal College of Art, after which he moved to Tel Aviv and joined the Studia group. His current collaboration with the IDEO group began in San Fransisco but he also worked for them in Japan where their clients included NEC, Seiko and Matsushita. He won the D&AD Exhibition Category Award in 1998 for his White Box Design and then moved to London where he is head of industrial design at IDEO. He lectures in Japan and his work forms part of the permanent collection of MoMA, New York. 39, 100, 101, 184, 185

Hans Heisz was born in Vienna in 1947. He has had many occupations including carpenter, mechanical engineer as well as pursuing the study of music. Since 1985 he has concentrated on his artistic activities and has recently worked with Anthologie Quartett on a lighting project. His areas of work are design, music, ceramics and graphics. 91

Scott Henderson was born in 1966 and lives in New York where he is Director of Industrial Design for Smart Design. He has lectured on design internationally and his work is held in the permanent collection of the Cooper-Hewitt National Design Museum and the Chicago Athenaeum. 191

Yas Hirai was born in Osaka, Japan in 1961 and studied furniture design at the Royal College of Art, London. He worked for IDEO Product Development in the US for some years and since 2000 he has been Associate Professor of Industrial Design at the Kyushu Institute of Design in Fukuoka, Japan. 22

Yoshiki Hishinuma was born in Sendai City, Japan in 1958. He studied at Bunka College of Fashion and then worked for the Issey Miyake design studio before setting up as a freelance designer, specializing in costume. In the 1980s he became known for his uniquely shaped clothes, which often employed wind and air. In 1992 he produced his own line of clothing and began showing his collections in Paris. In 1996 he was awarded the Mainichi Prize for Fashion for using technology to reinvigorate traditional Japanese tie-dye designs. 95, 96–7, 130

Richard Hutten was born in the Netherlands in 1967 and is a founder member of Droog Design. He graduated from the Design Academy of Eindhoven in 1991 and set up his own design studio in Rotterdam, working on furniture, industrial design and interior design. Among his clients are Hidden, Sawaya & Moroni, Idée, S.M.A.K., Pure Design, Karl Lagerfeld and HRH Queen Beatrix. 148, 149

David Huycke is a gold and silversmith. He was born in Sint-Niklaas, Belgium in 1967 where he now lives and works. Since graduating from the Karel de Grote-Hogeschool, Antwerp in 1989 he has combined teaching with his own metalwork and has exhibited in Belgium and Paris. His work is held in the collections of museums

in Belgium and France and has won various prizes, including the under 35s European Prize for Contemporary Art and Design Led Crafts in 1998. 18, 19

James Irvine was born in London in 1958. After studying industrial design at Kingston Polytechnic and the Royal College of Art, he moved to Milan where he was a design consultant for Olivetti, working under the direction of Michele De Lucchi and Ettore Sottsass. In 1988 he moved to the Toshiba Design Centre in Tokyo but returned to Milan to open his own studio whose clients have included Cappellini, BRF and SCP. Irvine was a partner in Sottsass Associati from 1993 to 1998. In 1999 he completed the design of the new city bus for USTRA, the Hanover transport system. Current clients include Artemide, B&B Italia, Magis, Canon Inc. and Arabia, Finland. 74

Claudy Jongstra was born in the Netherlands in 1963 and studied fashion and textiles in Utrecht. She set up Not Tom, Dick & Harry in 1990 and since then has developed a diverse client list which includes John Galliano, Star Wars 'The Phantom Menace', Donna Karan, Volvo and Bruce Weber. She has exhibited in the Netherlands, France, the UK, Italy and the USA, while her work is held in the collections of museums in The Hague, Amsterdam, London and New York. 105, 119, 121, 125

Toshiyuka Kita was born in Osaka in 1942 and graduated in industrial design from the Naniwa College in 1964. He established his own design studio in Osaka and began working both in Milan and Japan focusing on domestic environments and interior design. In 1989 he was presented with the Delta de Oro Award in Spain. He designed the interiors and chairs for the rotating theatre in the Japanese Pavilion at Expo '92, Seville. He is a visiting lecturer at the Hochschule für Angewandte Kunst in Vienna and has founded a private school in the Fukui Prefecture of Japan. 202–3

Komplot Design was founded in 1987 by Poul Christiansen and Boris Berlin. They are active in the fields of industrial, graphic and furniture design. Poul Christiansen was born in Copenhagen in 1947, where he studied architecture at the Royal Academy of Fine Arts. Boris Berlin was born in St Petersburg in 1953, where he studied at the Institute of Applied Arts and Design. He moved to Denmark in 1983 and since then Komplot Design has exhibited widely in Europe and Asia. They have won many awards in Scandinavia and their work is in the permanent collection of the Danish Museum of Decorative Art. 163

Nel Linssen is a Dutch jewellery designer. Based in Amsterdam, she specializes in intricately folded pieces made from reinforced paper. Her work has featured in exhibitions in London and New York. 152

Piero Lissoni was born in 1956. He studied architecture at Milan Polytechnic and then worked for G14 studio, Molteni and Lema. In 1984 he formed his own company with Nicoletta Canesi, working on product, graphic, interior, industrial and architectural projects. Since 1996 he has worked with Boffi Cucine as Art Director and in 1987 he began to collaborate with Porro, Living Design and Matteograssi. After working in Japan in the early 1990s, Lissoni was appointed Art Director for Lema and then in 1995, for Cappellini. In 1998 he began a collaboration with Benetton. Since then he has worked on various interior design projects including the headquarters of Welondfa, two new show-rooms for Cappellini, the Allegri showroom and the Boffi Bagna showroom in Milan. 41

Uta Majmudar is a glass artist. She was born in Berlin in 1935 and after university worked for some years as a school teacher. In 1978 she took up studies at the technical glass school in Hadamar and from 1986 to 1988 studied at the State Academy Aachen. She has had her own studio since 1980 and her work is held in the collections of museums throughout Europe. 63

Ingo Maurer is globally acclaimed for his innovative lighting designs. Born in 1932 on the island of Reichnau, Lake Constance, Germany, he trained in typography and graphic design. In 1960 he moved to the USA and worked as a freelance designer in San Francisco and New York before returning to Europe in 1963. Maurer founded Design M in Munich in 1966 and since then has achieved worldwide recognition. He has exhibited widely and his work forms part of the major collections in many museums, including MoMA, New York. 70, 71

Alberto Meda was born in Italy in 1945 and studied mechanical engineering at Milan Polytechnic. In 1973 he took up the position of Technical Director at Kartell and from 1979 was consultant designer and engineer for Alias, Brevetti, CSI Colomo Design and Swatch Italia. Meda was project director at Alfa Romeo from 1981 to 1985 and Professor of Production Technology at the Domus Academy, Milan from 1983 to 1987. He has been awarded the Compasso d'Oro twice, in 1989 and in 1994. In 1999 he was named Createur de l'Anée. Three of his chair designs for Alias are in the permanent collection of MoMA, New York. Meda is currently Professor at the Domus Academy and lectures at Milan Polytechnic. 52–3, 98

Thomas Meyerhoffer is a Swedish-born industrial designer. Having worked for Porsche, IDEO and Apple, he led the team which designed the first transluscent computer, the Apple eMate. In 1998 he founded Meyerhoffer Studios in California and their diverse client list includes Nike, Ericsson and Orrefors. The studio is currently developing sport, furniture, glass and technology objects. Thomas Meyerhoffer has received numerous awards, while his work is widely published and held in the permanent collection of the San Francisco Museum of Modern Art. 208

Massimo Micheluzzi was born in 1957 and studied Art History at the Ca' Foscari University in Venice. He then worked for the great Murano glassmaking family, Venini. In 1980 he began producing Laura de Santillana's work and subsequently worked with one of the great glass masters, Archimede Seguso. These experiences led him to start working glass himself and the result is a unique combination of artistic knowledge and sensibility. He has a studio in Venice. 65

Ritsue Mishima was born in Kyoto, Japan in 1962 and moved to Milan in 1982 where she was a freelance stylist for advertising and interior design magazines. She moved to Venice in 1989 and since 1995 has been designing glass objects, collaborating with the glass blowers of Murano. Her work has been shown in Milan, London and Tokyo and she recently won a Giorgio Armani award for her participation in an event organized by Sotheby's called 'Contemporary Decorative Arts'. 76

Carlo Moretti was born in Murano in 1934 and today lives in Venice. He attended law school in Padua, then in 1958 established the Carlo Moretti company with his brother Giovanni. They work in Murano crystal and their work can be found in major museums

in Europe and the US. Carlo Moretto is the sole administrator of Immobiliare Murano SRL, which opened the Contemporary Museum of Glass in Murano. 64

Jasper Morrison was born in London in 1959. He studied design at Kingston Polytechnic and undertook postgraduate work at the Royal College of Art, London and the Hochschule der Kunste, Berlin. In 1986 he set up his Office for Design in London, since which time he has worked for Alessi, Alias, Cappellini, Flos, Magis, SCP, Rosenthal and Vitra. In 1995 his office was awarded the contract to design the new Hannover tram for Expo 2000. Recent projects have included furniture for London's Tate Modern gallery. 182, 183

Ted Muehling studied industrial design at the Pratt Institute, New York but subsequently moved into jewellery design. He is inspired by organic forms found in nature and his work aims to embody a combination of craftsmanship and intuition. More recently he has diversified into wood, glass and porcelain and is currently working with the Italian company, Salviati. 72

Gabriela Nahlikova has worked with Leona Matejkova since 1996. Both attended the Academy of Art, Architecture and Design in Prague, studying under the designer Borek Sipek. Nahlikova spent a further year at the Academie Bellende Kunsten in Maastricht. Their work has been exhibited across Europe to much acclaim. 172

Marc Newson is from Sydney, Australia where he studied jewellery and sculpture. He started experimenting in furniture design at college and moved to Japan in 1987. In 1991 he moved to Paris where he set up a studio working for clients such as Moroso and Cappellini. Since the mid-1990s he has become increasingly involved in interior design and has worked on restaurants such as Coast in London, Mash and Air in Manchester and Osman in Cologne. In 1997 he moved to London and started Marc Newson Ltd, since which time he has designed a wide range of items for Alessi, Ittalia, Magis and Flos. 31

Patrick Norguet was born in 1969 and graduated from the Ecole Supérieure de Design Industriel. He works in stage design, interior architecture and product design and his clients include Louis Vuitton, Lanvin, L'Oreal, Cappellini and Martine Sitbon. 136–7

Fabio Novembre was born in Italy in 1966. He trained as an architect and now lives and works in Milan. He is best known for his imaginative interiors for bars, shops and restaurants. Recent work has included a hotel in Sardinia, a shop in New York and a showroom in Bisazza. He is also active in the field of product design and has collaborated with Cappellini. 135

Studio Olgoj Chorchoj was founded by Michal Fronek (b.1966) and Jan Nemecek (b.1963) in 1990, while they were studying at the Prague Academy of Arts, Architecture and Design. Presently they are in charge of the product design studio at the Academy. Studio Olgoj Chorchoj works on architecture, interior design, furniture, product design and jewellery. 78

Ann Pamintuan's company, The Gilded Expressions, makes elegant yet functional pieces in iron and alloys. Pamintuan draws her inspiration from the Japanese arts of ikebana and bonsai. In 1991, after a period as an ikebana trainer/demonstrator, she took a course in electroplating and began to experiment in covering plant specimens with metal. In 1992 she launched her first Gilded

Expressions jewellery collection in Manila. Since then, the line has expanded to include both functional and decorative objects and she has exhibited across Asia, Europe and the US. Recently, Gilded Expressions was nominated for the UNESCO Asian Product Design Collection Award. 15, 20

Verner Panton was born in Denmark in 1926. He studied at Copenhagen's Royal Academy of Fine Arts and then worked as an independent architect and designer. In the early 1960s he moved to Switzerland and his Panton chair became one of the best known pieces of the twentieth century. He also worked in interior design, lighting and textiles. A fellow of the Royal Society of Arts, Panton died in 1998. Major retrospectives were held at the Design Museum in 1999 and the Vitra Design Museum, Weil am Rhein in 2000. 133

Floyd Paxton was born in London in 1959. He studied design and is now based in Amsterdam where he works in the fields of interior and product design as well as photography. Since 1996 he has worked for Serien Raumleuchten GmbH. 94

Stephen Peart was born in Durham, England in 1958 and studied industrial design at Sheffield City Polytechnic followed by an MA from the Royal College of Art, London. In 1987, after working as design director for Frogdesign he established his own design consultancy, Vent, in California. Clients have included Apple Computers, Nike, Herman Miller, Knoll and Jetstream. 204

Roberto Pezzetta was born in Treviso in 1946. After periods in the design departments of Zoppas and Nordica he moved to Zanussi where he has been head of the Industrial Design Centre since 1982. He has won many awards including the Compasso d'Oro in 1981 and since 1993 has been the Director of Design for the Electrolux Design Management Team. 40

Ferdinand Alexander Porsche was born in Stuttgart in 1935. After an apprenticeship with Porsche, he attended the design school in Ulm and in 1958 began working for Porsche. He was involved in the development of the Porsche '904' and the '911' and in 1968 became deputy manager of Porsche KG. In 1972 he founded Porsche Design and in 1999 was awarded an honorary Professorship by Vienna University. 28, 29

Ingegerd Råman is a celebrated Swedish glass designer and ceramicist. She was born in 1943 and studied in the UK, Sweden and Italy. Initially she worked for Joyhansfors Glasbruk AB, then Skrufs Glasbruk AB. Since 1999 she has worked for Orrefors Glasbruk but she has also had her own studio since 1972. She has consistently won awards for her work and is represented in museums in Europe and the USA. In 1999 the American Craft Museum in New York held an exhibition of her work. 61

Karim Rashid was born in Cairo in 1960 and graduated in industrial design from Carleton University in Ottowa, Canada in 1982. After graduate studies in Italy he moved to Milan, then returned to Canada where he worked with KAN Industrial Designers for seven years. Rashid was a full-time associate professor of industrial design at the University of Arts in Philadelphia for six years and also taught at the Pratt Institute, the Rhode Island School of Design and Ontario College of Art. Since 1992 he has been principal designer for Karim Rashid Industrial Design in New York and has won many awards including the 1999 George Nelson Award and the Silver IDEA

Award for the Oh Chair. His work has been exhibited in MoMA, New York, the Chicago Athenaeum and the Design Museum, London. 128, 129, 186, 187, 189, 200

Aaron Rincover studied architecture at Washington State University, graduating in 1994. He is currently studying digital media design in Pasadena. He has worked on various projects, ranging from architecture to web design and product design. He has recently collaborated with the London-based lighting company, Mathmos. In 2001 he was awarded the Red Dot Award 'Best of the Best' and the IDSA Bronze Medal. 174, 175

Eric Robin was born in Mâcon in 1968 and studied at the National Art School, Dijon and the Decorative Art School, Paris. Based in Paris since 1990, he works alone or in collaboration with designers such as Christian Ghion and Eric Gizard. 124

Vibeke Rohland is a Danish textile designer. After initially reading art history at the University of Copenhagen, she studied textiles at the School of Art and Craft in Copenhagen. ELIAKIM (Création de Tissus) in Paris provided her with several years experience before returning to Denmark where she has continued to work, teach and exhibit regularly. Her clients have included international companies such as Esprit and Agnès B. 127

Marco Romanelli was born in Trieste in 1958. He has been collaborating with Marta Laudani since 1986 but also works independently from his studio in Rome. He has been art director of O Luce since 1995 and of Montina since 1996. From 1994 to 1997 he was a consultant for Driade. He has been on the editorial staff of Abitare since 1995 and in 2000 he organized the third 'Aperto Vetro' section of the Venice Biennale Exhibition. 56, 57

Sonia Rykiel is an internationally distinguished fashion designer. She was born in Paris in 1930 and despite lacking formal training, opened her first boutique in Saint Germain in 1968. She immediately earned a cult following for her knitwear and long, lean style which endures to this day. Although she is known primarily for her work in fashion, Rykiel is also active in the fields of literature, theatre and gastronomy. 212

Timo Salli was born in Porvoo, Finland in 1963. Initially he worked as a welder before enrolling at the Lahti Design Institute and later the University of Art and Design. In 1993 he founded his studio, Muotoilutomisto Salli Ltd and since then he has operated independently or in collaboration with product design groups such as Snowcrash and Sitra. 54, 55

Takahide Sano studied industrial design in Tokyo. From 1976 until 1988 he worked for the Toshiba Design Centre, since which time he has been freelance. Collaborations have included WMF, Nishimura Plastics and Sottsass Associati. He has won several awards and has taught in Milan and Antwerp. 44, 45

Christian Schwamkrug was born in Düsseldorf in 1957. He studied industrial design at the University of Wuppertal and then freelanced for several years. Since 1987 he has worked as a designer for Porsche in Zell am See, Austria. 28, 29

Jerszy Seymour was born in 1968 in Berlin and graduated in engineering design from the South Bank Polytechnic of London in 1989. He then took an MA in industrial design at the Royal College of Art. Now based in Milan, he has worked for companies such as Magis, Idée Japan Co. Ltd, Sutnik, BRF, Swatch and Smeg. His work has been shown at the Centre Pompidou in Paris and in various exhibitions in Milan, New York, Tokyo and Berlin. He was visiting Professor at the Domus Academy and won the Daedalus Award for European Design in 2000. 75

Yashushi Shiotani was born in Tokyo in 1962. He studied product design at the University of Tsukuba and received an MA from the Domus Academy in Milan in 1993. He now works in the camera design group at Canon Inc. and received the Red Dot award for Highest Design Quality for the 'Ixus' camera in 1997. He has lectured in both Italy and the USA. 209

Michael Sodeau studied product design at Central Saint Martins College of Art & Design in London. He was a founding partner of Inflate in 1995 but left in 1997 to set up a partnership with Lisa Giuliani. He launched his first collection of furniture and homeware in 1997. Current clients include Gervasoni. 159

Sarah Taylor is a lecturer in visual studies at Heriot-Watt University in Scotland. She graduated in textile design from Winchester School of Art in 1991 and completed an MPhil at Heriot-Watt in 1995 for her research into fibre optic technology and textiles. She has exhibited widely and has recently collaborated with the British fashion designer, Helen Storey. 106, 107

Lotte Thorsoe is a Danish glassmaker. In 1995, after apprenticeships in the UK and Denmark, she enrolled at the Design School in Kolding, from which she graduated in 2000. She designs for Holmegard Factory, Royal Scandinavia and also works freelance. 77

Michael Toepffer was born in Germany in 1958. From 1978 to 1981 he served a carpenter's apprenticeship followed by a diploma. Until 1994 he worked freelance in Aachen, then he undertook further study at the Academy of Craft and Design. Since graduating in 1997, he has worked freelance and undertook a study residence at Donald Judd's Chinati Foundation, Marfa, Texas, in 1998. 146

Kazuhiko Tomita was born in 1965 in Nagasaki, Japan. He gained a BEng in industrial design at Chiba University and in 1990 won a Cassina scholarship to study furniture design at the Royal College of Art, London. He was awarded first prize in the 'Architectural Future of Stainless Steel' competition and the MA RCA Marchette Award for his degree work 'Hadakano Piano, aria'. He has exhibited frequently at the Milan Furniture Fair as well as Abitare Il Tempo. Recent projects have included tableware ranges for Covo. 17

David Trubridge was born in Oxford, England in 1951. After studying naval architecture at Newcastle University he self-trained in woodwork. As a self-employed craftsman he undertook commissions for the Victoria & Albert Museum and Saint Mary's Cathedral, Edinburgh, amongst others. From 1982 until 1986 he and his family sailed a yacht to New Zealand, building furniture in the Caribbean and Tahiti en route. Since then he has exhibited across the world and his work is manufactured by Cappellini. In 2001 he formed the group Pacific Edge to exhibit in Milan. He also writes, lectures and teaches in art, craft and design. 164

Paolo Ulian was born in 1961 and studied painting in Carrara followed by industrial design in Florence. From 1990 to 1992 he worked as an assistant at Enzo Mari's studio, then founded Paolo Ulian Industrial Design. He has exhibited widely and collaborates with companies such as Driade, Segno, Progetto and Zani&Zani. 60, 142, 143

Roderick Vos was born in the Netherlands in 1965 and studied industrial design in Eindhoven. He worked for Kenji Ekuans GK in Tokyo and Ingo Maurer in Munich before founding his own studio, Studio Maupertuus, with Claire Vos-Teeuwen. Their client portfolio includes Espaces et Lignes, Driade, Authentics and Alessi, while their work has been shown at the Milan, Cologne and New York Furniture Fairs. 46, 47

Marcel Wanders was born in the Netherlands in 1963. He studied at various colleges of design in the Netherlands and in 1995 established his own studio, Wanders' Wonders. His numerous clients have included Cappellini, Droog Design, Habitat, Mandarina Duck and British Airways. In 2000 Wanders established Moooi, a production company dedicated to embracing those whose work is deemed too unconventional. Wanders is art director and head designer. His work is held in museums throughout Europe and the USA. 14, 66, 158, 168

Carol Westfall studied at the Rhode Island School of Design and the Maryland Institute College of Art before commencing postgraduate studies at the Kawashima Textile School, Kyoto. She also spent time studying in Mexico and India. She is now a Professor of Fine Arts at Montclair State University and lectures and exhibits throughout the world. Her work is held in many museum collections. 112, 113

Hannes Wettstein works in product design, corporate design, interior design and architecture. He was born in Switzerland in 1958 and started out as a freelance designer. He then joined the Eclat Agency as a partner. In 1993 he co-founded 9D Design and also teaches, having held a professorial chair in Karlshule since 1994. He has won many awards and notable projects include the Swiss Embassy in Tehran and the Grand Hyatt Hotel in Berlin. His varied list of clients includes Cassina, UMS Pastoe, Shimano, Baleri Italia and Artemide. 192, 193

Robert Wettstein is a self-taught designer. Born in Zurich in 1960, he has been active in furniture and lighting design since 1985. He has collaborated with companies such as Structure Design, Anthologie Quartett, Zeus, Authentics and DIM. 147

Theo Williams was born in Oxford in 1967. He studied in Bristol and Manchester and graduated in industrial design in 1990. He works as a freelance designer and has collaborated with companies such as Technogym Italia, Nava Design and Pyrex Europe. Williams has developed products for Prada, Armani, Calvin Klein and Tronconi and has recently designed a range of products for Lexon, France, where he is Art Director. 206

Tokujin Yoshioka was born in Japan in 1967. He graduated from the Kuwasawa Design School in 1986 and subsequently worked for Issey Miyake. Since 1992 he has operated freelance and counts BMW, Shiseido and NTT-X among his clients. In 2000 he established Tokujin Yoshioka Design and won the I.D. Annual Design Award for Excellence in both 2000 and 2001. 23, 198

Suppliers

Alessi SpA, Via Privata Alessi 6, 28882 Crusinallo (VB), Italy. T. +39 (0)323 868611 F. +39 (0)323 641605 E. info@alessi.com W. www.alessi.com

Alias SpA, Via dei Videtti 2, Grumello del Monte (Bergamo), Italy. T. +39 035 4422 511 E. info@aliasdesign.it W. www.aliasdesign.it

Anthologie Quartett, Schloss Huennefeld, 49152 Bad Essen, Germany. T. +49 (0)5472 940 90 F. +49 (0)5472 940 940 W. www.anthologiequartett.de

Aptero Oy, Kauppalantie 12, FIN-02700 Kauniainen, Finland. T. +358 950505598 F. + 358 954752535 W. www.aptero.com

Designor Oy Ab Arabia, Hämeentie 135, FIN-00560 Helsinki, Finland. T. +358 204 3911 F. +358 204 39 57 41 E. arabia.info@designor.com W. www.arabia.fi

Arcade Glass E. info@arcadeglass.com W. www.arcadeglass.com

Artemide SpA, Via Canova 34, Milan 20145, Italy. T. +39 (0)234 96 11 F. +39 (0)234 53 82 11 E. pr@artemide.com W. www.artemide.com

Atrox GmbH, Seeblick 1, Cham CH-6330, Switzerland. T. (0) 41 785 0410 F. +41 785 0419 E. info@atrox-gmbh.ch W. www.atrox-gmbh.ch

Audi AG, Kundenbetreuung Deutschland, Postfach 100457, 85004 Ingolstadt, Germany. T. 0800 2834 7378423 F. 0800 329 262834 W. www.audi.com

Jacob de Baan, Nieuwevaart 128, 1018 ZM Amsterdam, the Netherlands. T. +31 20 7760018 F. +31 20 7760019 E. info@jacobdebaan.com W. www.jacobdebaan.com

B&B Italia, Strada Provinciale 32, 22060 Novedrate (CO), Italy. T. +39 031 795 111 F. +39 031 791 592 W. www.bebitalia.it

Blue Project Team, Via Guariento 5, Bassano del Grappa 36061 (VI), Italy. T. +39 0424 505205 F. +39 0424 508217

Bonacina, Via S. Andrea 20A, I-22040 Lurago D' Erba (CO), Italy. T. +39 031 699225 E.bonacina@bonacinapierantonio.it W. www.bonacinapierantonio.it

Debbie Jane Buchan, 3 Hutchinson Avenue, Edinburgh EH14 1Q8, Scotland

Bulo Belgium, Industriezone Noord B6, B-2800 Mechelen, Belgium. T. +32 (0)15 28 28 28 F. +32 (0)15 28 28 29 E. info@bulo.be W. www.bulo.be

Canon Inc. Design Centre, 3-30-2 Shimomaruko, Ohta-Ku, 146-8501 Tokyo, Japan. T. +81 3 3758 2111 F. +81 3 5482 9852 W. www.canon.co.jp

Cappellini SpA, Via Marconi 35, 22060 Arosio (CO), Italy. T. +39 031759111 F. +39 031763322 E. cappellini@cappellini.it W. www.cappellini.it

Casimir®, Guido Gezellelaan 169, 3550 Heusden-Zolder, Belgium. T +32 11 45 25 35 F. +32 11 43 22 14 E. info@casimir.be W. www.casimir.be

Jean-Charles de Castelbajac, 15 rue Cassette, 75006 Paris, France. T. +33 1 53 63 14 14 F. +33 1 42 22 83 33

Catellani & Smith, Via Antonio Locatelli 47, 24020 Villa di Serio (BG), Italy. T. +39 035 656 088 F. +39 035 655 695 E. info@catellanismith.com W. www.catellanismith.com

Counterpoint, 2626 North Stanton, El Paso, Texas 79902, USA. T. +1 915 545 5073 F. +1 915 545 5076 W. www.counterpoint1.com

Covo srl, Via degli Olmetti 3/b, 00060 Formello (Rome), Italy. T. +39 06 90400311 F. +39 06 90409175 E. mail@covo.it W. www.covo.it

Danskina, Pakhuis Amsterdam, Oostelijke Handelskade 15–17, 1019 BL Amsterdam, the Netherlands. T. +31 (0) 20 4198586 F. +31 (0) 20 4198601 E. orga@danskina.nl W. www.danskina.nl

Digital Reflection, Inc., 644 University Avenue, Los Gatos, 95030 CA, USA. T. +1 408 313 6340 F. +1 408 559 4036

Droog Design, Sarphatikade 11, 1017 WV Amsterdam, the Netherlands. T. +31 (0) 20 62 69 809 +31 F. (0) 20 63 88 828 E. info@droogdesign.nl W. www.droogdesign.nl

Dyson Ltd, Tetbury Hill, Malmesbury, Wiltshire, SN16 ORP, UK. T. +44 01666 827 200 F. +44 01666 827 299 E. service@dyson.com W. www.dyson.com

Edra SpA, Via Livornese Est 106, Perignano 56030 (PI), Italy. T. +39 (0) 587 61 66 60 F. +39 (0) 587 61 75 00 E. edra@edra.com W. www.edra.com

Electrolux Zanussi SpA, Via Giardini Cattaneo 3, 33170 Pordenone, Italy. T. +39 0434 396 210 F. +39 0434 396 045 W. www.electrolux.it

Eleksen Limited (Electrotextiles), Pinewood Studios, Pinewood Road, Iver Heath, Bucks SLO ONH, UK. T. +44 (0)8700 727272 F. +44 (0)8700 727273 W. www.electrotextiles.com

Ennemlaghi Ltd, 10 Palmerston Road, London N22 8RG, UK. T. +44 (0)207 987 3945 F. +44 (0)207 987 3945 E. ennemlaghi@europe.com W. www.ennemlaghi.com

Eoos, Theresieng 11/15, A-1180 Vienna, Austria. T. +43 1 405 3987 F. +43 1 405 3987 80 E. design@eoos.com W. www.eoos.com

Ericsson Sverige AB, Lindhagensgatan 80, 12625 Stockholm, Sweden. T. +46 8 579 180 00 F. +46 8 579 180 01 W. www.ericsson.se

Felicerossi, Via Sempione 17, 21011 Casorate Sempione (VA), Italy. T. +39 0331 767131 F. +39 0331 768449 E. info@felicerossi.it W. www.felicerossi.it

Ferlea, Zona Industriale San Marziale, 53034 Colle Val d' Elsa, Siena, Italy. T. +39 0577 929400 F. +39 0577 928092 E. ferlea@ferlea.com W. www.ferlea.com

Flos SpA, Via Angelo Faini 2, 25073 Bovezzo (BS), Italy. T. +39 0302 4381 F. +39 0302 438250 E. info@flos.it W. www.flos.net

Fuji Photo Film Co. Ltd, 26–30 Nishiazabu 2-chome, J-106-8620 Tokyo, Japan. T. +81 3 3406 2728 F. +81 3 3406 2666 E. isozaki@tokyo.fujifilm.co.jp W. www.fujifilm.co.jp

Fusina snc, Via Rivarotta 1, Bassano del Grappa (Vicenza), Italy. T. +39 0424 590 634 F. +39 0424 829 930 E. luca@fusina-italy.com

Jean-Marc Gady, 52 rue des Abbesses, 75018 Paris, France. T. +33 (0)1 46 06 8134 E. jmgady@club-internet.fr

Gervasoni SpA, Zone Industriale Udinese, 33050 Pavia di Udine, Italy. T. +39 0432 656611 F. +39 0432 656612 E. info@gervasoni1882.com W. www.gervasoni1882.com

The Gilded Expressions, Apo View Hotel, Davao City 8000, Philippines. T. +63 82 221 6430 F. +63 82 221 0748 E. gildex@mozcom.com

Gruppe RE, Gottesweg 173, 50939 Cologne, Germany. T. +49 (0)221 95 45 101 E. mail@gruppe-re.de W. www.gruppe-re.de

Isabel Hamm, Gocher Strasse 29, 50733 Cologne, Germany. T. +49 (0)221 7391492 F. +49 (0)221 7391493 E. Isabel.Hamm@t-online.de W. www.isabel-hamm.de

Herbst LaZar Bell, 355 North Canal Street, Chicago, IL 60606, USA. T. +1 312 454 1116 F. +1 312 454 9019 W. www.hlb.com

Hidden, SDB Industries BV, De Beverspijken 20, 5221 ED, 's Hertogenbosch, The Netherlands. T. +31 736 339 133 F. +31 736 312 422 E. info@sdb-industries.nl

Hishinuma Associates Co. Ltd, Tokyo, Japan. T. +81 (0)3 5770 8333 F. +81 (0)3 5770 8334 W. www.yoshikihishinuma.co.jp

David Huycke, Bekelstraat 160, B-9100 Sint-Niklaas, Belgium. T. +32 (0) 477 805 482 F. +32 (0) 3766 5612

Inflate, 11 Northburgh Street, London EC1V OAH, UK. T. +44 (0)20 7251 5453 F. +44 (0)20 7250 0311 E. info@inflate.co.uk W. www.inflate.co.uk

Interior Crafts of the Islands, Inc., 3-A Gen. Maxilom Ave., Cebu City 6000, Philippines. T. +63 32 233 3056 F. +63 32 231 2555 E. ici@cebu.pw.net.ph

Isaksson Gruppen AB, Box 203, 566–24 Habo, Sweden. T. +46 (0) 36 484 00 F. +46 (0) 36 414 55 W. www.isakssongruppen.se

Källemo, Box 605, S-331 26 Varnamo, Sweden. T. +46 (0) 370 150 00 F. +46 (0) 370 150 60 E. info@kallemo.se W. www.kallemo.se

Kopf Solardesign GmbH & Co. Kg, Stutzenstrabe 6, D-72172 Sulz Bersfelden, Germany. T. +49 (0) 7454 75 288 F. +49 (0) 7454 75 302 E. info@kopf-solardesign.com W. www.kopf-solardesign.com

KorQinc, 155 East 56th Street, New York, NY 10022, USA. T. +1 212 758 2593 F. +1 212 758 0025 E. info@korqinc.com W. www.korqinc.com

Lexon, 98 Boulevard Hêloise, 95100 Argenteuil, France. T. +33 1 39 47 0400 F. +33 1 39 47 07 59 W. www.lexon-design.com

LG Electronics UK Ltd, LG House, 264 Bath Road, Slough, Berkshire SL1 4DT, UK. T. +44 0870 607 5544 W. www.lge.com

Luminara, Viale Sicilia 4, Cascina – Pisa 56021, Italy. T. +39 050 711 289 F. +39 050 700 872 E. info@luminara.it W. www.luminara.it

Magis srl, Via Magnadola 15, 31045 Motta di Livenza (Treviso), Italy. T. +39 0422 768 742 F. +39 0422 766 395 E. magisuno@tin.it

Maharam, 251 Park Avenue South, New York NY 10010, USA. T. +1 212 614 2900 F. +1 212 995 0349 W. www.maharam.com

Uta Majmudar, Glasgestalterin, Mozartstrasse 27, 42781 Haan, Germany. T. +49 (0)2129 6117 F. +49 (0) 2129 329 08

Massimo Lunardon & Snc, Via Motarello 6, 36060 Molvena (VI), Italy. T. +39 0424 708329 F. +39 0424 708329

Mathmos Ltd, 20 Old Street, London EC1V 9AP, UK. T. +44 (0)20 7549 2700 F. +44 (0)20 7549 2745 E. mathmos@mathmos.co.uk W. www.mathmos.com

Massimo Micheluzzi, Dorsoduro 1071, 30123 Venice, Italy. T/F. +39 041 5282190 E. maravege@tin.it

Issey Miyake, 5 Place des Vosges, 75005 Paris, France. T. +33 (0)1 4454 5600 F. +33 (0)1 4277 3808 W. www.isseymiyake.com

Molteni & C. SpA, Via Rossini 50, 20034 Giussano (Milan), Italy. T. +39 0362 3591 F. +39 0362 354448 E. customer.service@molteni.it W. www.molteni.it

Money For Milan, Mariannenplatz 1, Munich 80538, Germany. T. +49 89 2285262 F. +49 89 2285714 E. info@moneyformilan.com W. www.moneyformilan.com

Moooi©, Jacob Catskade 35, 1052 BT Amsterdam, The Netherlands. T. +31 20 6815051 F. +31 20 6815056 E. info@moooi.com W. www.moooi.com

Carlo Moretti srl, Fondamenta Manin, 30141 Murano (Venice), Italy. T. +39 041 739217 F. +39 041 736282

Gabriela Nahlikova, 12 u Uranie, 17000 Prague, Czech Republic. T. +420 287 6685 E. navassdva@hotmail.com

Nike, USA. W. www.nike.com

Not Tom Dick & Harry, Openhartsteeg 1, 1017 BD, Amsterdam, the Netherlands. T. +31 20 42 84 230 F. +31 20 62 09 673 E. NTDH@wxs.nl

Olgoj Chorchoj, Libensky Ostrov 1555, 180 00 Prague, Czech Republic. T/F. +420 268 3685 E. olgoj@mbox.vol.cz W. olgojchorchoj.cz

Orrefors Kosta Boda AB, SE 380 40 Orrefors, Sweden. T. +46 481 340 00 F. +46 481 303 50 W. www.orrefors.se

Produzione Privata, Via Giorgio Pallavicino 31, 20145 Milan, Italy. T. +39 02 43008209 F. +39 02 43008222 E. p.morgan@amdl.it W. www.produzioneprivata.it

Vibeke Rohland, Holbergsgade 19, 3, DK-1057 Copenhagen K, Denmark. T. +45 33 144406 E. mentalswimwear@c.dk

Rosendahl A/S, Maglebjergvej 4, DK-2800 Lyngby, Denmark. T. +45 4588 6633 F. +45 4593 1999 E. info@rosendahl.dk W. www.rosendahl.dk

Royal Leerdam, P.O. Box 8, 4140 AA Leerdam, the Netherlands. T. +31 (0)345 671611 F. +31 (0)345 610496 E. rl.info@royalleerdam.com W. www.royalleerdam.com

Royal van Kempen & Begeer, Zilverstraat 40, 2718 RK Zoetermeer, The Netherlands. T. +31 79 3680580 F. +31 79 3680579 E. info@kempen-begeer.nl W. www.kempen-begeer.nl

Rubinetterie Stella SpA, Via Unità d' Italia, 1-28100 Novara, Italy. T. +39 0321 473 351 F. +39 0321 474 231 E. info@rubinetteriestella.it W. www.rubinetteriestella.it

Sonia Rykiel, 175 Boulevard St Germain, 75006 Paris, France. T. +33 (0)1 49546060 W. www.soniarykiel.com

Timo Salli, Muotoilutoimisto Salli Ltd. Meritullinkatu 11, FIN-00170 Helsinki, Finland. T. +358 968137700 F. +358 92782277 E. salli@timosalli.com

Salviati, Fondamenta Radi 16, I-30141 Murano (Venice), Italy. T. +39 041 527 4085 F. +39 041 527 5348 E. info@salviati.com W. www.salviati.com

Sawaya & Moroni SpA, Via Manzoni 11, Milan 20121, Italy. T. +39 (0)2 8639 5210 F. +39 (0)2 8646 4831 E. sawaya-moroni@apm.it W. www.sawayamoroni.com

Serafino Zani srl, Via Bosca 24/26, 25066 Lumezzane Gazzolo (Brescia), Italy. T. +39 030 871861 F. +39 030 8970620 W. www.serafinosani.it E. info@serafinozani.it

Serien Raumleuchten GmbH, Hainhäuser Strasse 3–7, D-63110 Rodgau, Germany. T. +49 (0)6106/69090 F. +49 (0)6106/690922 E. serien@serien.com W. www.serien.com

Sharp Corporation, Nagaike-cho 22–22, Abeno-Ku 545–8522, Japan. T. +81 6 6621 3637 F. +81 6 6629 6621 E. nisikawa@cdc.osa.sharp.co.jp W. www.sharp.co.jp

Smart Design, 137 Varick Street, New York, NY 10013, USA. T. +1 212 807 8150 F. +1 212 243 8514 E. info@smartdesignusa.com W. www.smartdesignusa.com

Stiletto Design Vertreib, Frank Schreiner, Augustrasse 2, D-10177 Berlin, Germany. T. +49 (0)30 427 3827 F. +49 (0)30 422 5750 W. www.stiletto.de

Structure Design, Josefstrasse 188, 8005 Zurich, Switzerland. T. +41 1272 9725 F. +41 1272 1717 E. otw@gmx.ch

Tarkett Sommer S.A., 2 rue de l'Egalité, F-92748 Nanterre Cedex, France. T. +33 (0)1 41 20 40 40 F. +33 (0)1 41 21 49 09 W. www.tarkett-sommer.com

Sarah Taylor, 2 The Wynd, Melrose TD6 9LD, Scottish Borders. T. +44 (0)1896 822133 F. +44 (0)1896 820136

Thomson Multimedia, 46 Quai Alphonse Le Gallo, 92648 Boulogne Cedex, France. T. +33 (0)1 41 86 50 00 F. +33 (0)1 41 86 58 59 W. thomsonmultimedia.com

Michael Toepffer, 71 Schrouf Strasse, 52078 Aachen, Germany. T. +49 (0)1798 450 3501 F. +49 (0)241 563921

Toshiba Corporation, 1-1 Shibaura, 1 Chome, Minato-ku, 105-8001 Tokyo, Japan. T. +81 3 3457 4022 F. +81 3 5444 9294 E. sakai@design.toshiba.co.jp W. www.toshiba.co.jp

David Trubridge, 44 Margaret Avenue, 4201 Havelock North, New Zealand. T. +64 6877 4684 E. trubridge@clear.net.nz W. www.davidtrubridge.com

Vitra AG, Klunenfeldstrasse 22, CH-127 Birsfelden, Switzerland. T +41 (0)61 377 1509 F. +41 (0)61 377 1510 E. info@vitra.com W. www.vitra.com

Yamaha Corporation, 10-1 Nakazawa Cho, Hamamatsu, Shikuoka Prefecture 430 8650, Japan. T. +81 (0)53 460 2883 F. +81 (0)53 4673 4992 W. www.yamaha.com

Tokujin Yoshioka, 9-1 Daikanyama-cho, Shibuya-ku, 150-0034 Tokyo, Japan. T. +81(0)3 54280830 F. +81(0)3 54280835 E. tokujin8@nifty.com

Photographic credits

The publisher and editors would like to thank the designers and manufacturers who submitted work for inclusion, and the following photographers and copyright holders for the use of their material (page numbers are given in parentheses):

Simone Barberis (90, 104 top & bottom, 120)
Yves Béhar/fuseproject (Design concept);
    Computer illustration: Geoffrey
    Petrizzi/fuseproject, Lisa Lo (58–9)
Jeoffrey Bello (173 bottom, 194 bottom, 195)
Markus Benesch (150, 151)
Bitetto E Chimenti (41, 168)
Boym Partners Inc. (110)
Erik Brahl (2, 163)
Erica Calvi (197)
Mimmo Capone (160, 161)
Marco Cavalmoretti (4, 88, 89)
Kenneth Cobonpue (154 top, 155)
© Peter Cook/View (5, 171)
Richard Davies (100, 101, 184, 185)
D. James Dee (112, 113)
Domus Editoriale SpA (128 bottom left,
    bottom right)
© Peter Durant/arcblue.com (5, 43)
Rick English (208)
Fredrik Eriksson (32 top)
Christophe Fillioux (128 top)
Kai Georg 2000 (91)
Walter Gumiero (136, 137)
Lars Gunderson (127)
Scott Henderson (191)
© Hiroyuki Hirai (5, 139)
David Huycke (18, 19)
Hiroshi Ikeba (209)
© Pentti Kokkanen/Flaming Star Ky (165)
Carlo Lavatori (74, 75, 76)
Massimo Micheluzzi (65)
Mads Mogensen (122 top & bottom)
Thomas de Monaco (212, 213)
© Nacása & Partners Inc. (198)
Augusto Naldoni (17)
Toine van den Nieuwendijk (80, 81)
Bart Nieuwenhuijs (123)
Ernst Noritz © Central Museum Utrecht (62)
Neil Oshima (154 bottom)
Andrés Otero (156 top & bottom, 157)
Roland Persson (1, 61)
Photos Tom Petrov, model Margaret F. Butler
    (210, 211)
Photo Tiziano (162)
Paul Prader (99 top & bottom)
© RISD Department of Furniture Design
    (126)
John Ross (5, 7, 8, 11, 87, 218–19)
Tiziano Rossi (44, 45)
Allan Rubin (186, 187)
Timo Salli (54, 55)
Salviati (67–73)
Maurice Scheltens (166 top & bottom)
Sharp Corporation Advertising Division (26,
    202–3, 205 top & bottom)
Young Sil Young (39)
Studio Synthesis (56, 57)
Goran Tacevski (78)
Peter Tahl (46, 47)
Peter Tang (164 top & bottom)
Sarah Taylor (106, 107)
Anna Tiedink (105, 119, 125)
Leo Torrí (214, 215)
Jason Tozer (180, 181)
Johannes Twielemeier (146)
Marcel van der Vlugt (121)
Verne (178, 179)
Uwe Walter (108, 109)
Allan Warnick (114, 118)
Lars Wivelsted (42, 77)
Bob Young (27)
Miro Zagnoli (84, 85)
Fabio Zonta (201)